Bill France Jr.

Bill France Jr.

The Man Who Made NASCAR

H.A. Branham

TRIUMPH
BOOKS

Library of Congress Cataloging-in-Publication Data

Branham, H. A.
  Bill France Jr. : the man who made NASCAR / H.A. Branham.
     p. cm.
  Includes index.
  ISBN 978-1-60078-340-1
  1. France, Bill Jr., 1933–1970. 2. NASCAR (Association)—Officials and employees—Biography. 3. Stock car racing—United States. 4. NASCAR (Association). I. Title.
  GV1032.F73B73 2009
  796.72092—dc22
  [B]
                              2010001798

This book is available in quantity at special discounts for your group or organization. For further information, contact:
  Triumph Books
  542 South Dearborn Street
  Suite 750
  Chicago, Illinois 60605
  (312) 939–3330
  Fax (312) 663–3557
  www.triumphbooks.com

Printed in U.S.A.
ISBN: 978-1-60078-340-1
Design by Patricia Frey
All photos courtesy of ISC Archives unless otherwise noted.

Contents

Foreword

Bill France Jr. was my kind of man.

He was equally at ease behind the wheel rocketing around a NASCAR track or atop a speeding motorcycle or at the gears of a backhoe. He was a marketing genius who turned a regional sport into a national passion and while he raced from track to track in a private jet, when he got back home to Daytona Beach, Florida, his idea of a four-star meal was a hamburger at a tiny cookout stand just off the Daytona International Speedway frontstretch.

Bill and I first met in the Seventies, when he was taking over NASCAR from his father, Bill Sr. I was visiting Daytona for the first time with my daughters, and I spent part of a memorable day with the two Bills.

They immediately strapped us into a pace car for a high-speed ride around the steeply banked oval while we talked racing and cars. I remember Bill Sr. suggesting we pool our money and buy several of the first generation Pontiac Firebirds that GM was phasing out. He said, "We'll just put them up on blocks and wait a few years, and they'll be worth a lot more."

I didn't follow up with him, but I came away impressed by the ease of the relationship between father and son, their common touch and common-sense approach to promoting America's longstanding love affair with cars and going fast.

When Bill Jr. took NASCAR to heights not even Big Bill could have imagined, I watched carefully to see if the son had been changed by his new fame and success.

He was still the same Bill Jr., a man of machines and simple tastes, a shrewd entrepreneur who understood that those fans in cut-offs and T-shirts crowding the infield were just as important to him, if not more so, than sponsors in the expensive suits and gold jewelry.

In fact, I once heard him speak disdainfully of a major sponsor who came to Daytona only to check on whether his product was getting the appropriate attention he felt it deserved. For Bill, NASCAR was first and last about the fans, the drivers, the cars, and the race.

When he was ill with what turned out to be terminal cancer, I called to ask a favor:

Could I bring a friend, a NASCAR fanatic, to Daytona for my friend's 40th birthday?

I fully expected Bill to turn us over to his staff, but there he was at the track, looking weary and a bit frail, the perfect host.

My friend was as thrilled with being a guest of Bill at Daytona as a golfer would have been to have Tiger Woods show him around Augusta.

We took a spin around the track, toured the fan attraction called the DAYTONA 500 Experience, looked at the statue of Dale Earnhardt, then retired for the birthday lunch to that tiny cookout stand and hamburgers on paper plates.

For my friend, it was the American dream come true, all arranged by a gifted and generous man who gave untold millions of Americans so much pleasure over so many years.

—Tom Brokaw

Acknowledgments

I got to know Bill France Jr. in the last five years of his life. In many ways he seemed to me a contrast to the man who had ruled NASCAR as a sometimes-benevolent dictator since the early 1970s. Age and illness had taken their respective, inevitable tolls. The Lion in Winter roared not nearly as often nor as loudly as in years past. That said, there were still plenty of vocal reminders of the good ol' days when NASCAR's drivers were still called the good ol' boys.

Suffice to say, then, that it was a *different* time in Bill's life. I was extremely lucky to be part of it, which my boss at NASCAR, Jim Hunter, reminded me one late-summer afternoon as we worked together on a draft of a speech Bill would be giving, a draft that Bill would of course partially rewrite to apply his own stamp on the finished product.

Technically, I was his speechwriter from 2002–07, but I am reluctant to use that title because when it came to those speeches, it most certainly was a collaboration. And so, let's just say that Bill and I "collaborated" on numerous speeches prior to his death. We worked closely, which helped me to understand a man who, for some, was hard to understand.

He also was a great help to me personally in the preparation and the promotion of two previous books I was fortunate enough to author—*The NASCAR Vault* and *The NASCAR Family Album*—even joining me for autograph signings, to the absolute surprise and delight of bookstore customers who were also NASCAR fans.

Now I wonder what he would say about this book. In writing it, I have tried to imagine he was still right down the hall from my office, that he might again appear in my doorway, holding a speech draft in his hands, not completely pleased with what he had read.

So many people have made this work possible, starting first and foremost with his wife of 50 years, Betty Jane France, who gave graciously of her time and memories.

There are many more to thank:

Bill's younger brother Jim, who relished the notion of Bill posthumously having the last word regarding a number of old issues and adversaries;

Bill and Betty Jane's children, Brian France and Lesa France Kennedy, now embellishing the family legacy as respective leaders of NASCAR and International Speedway Corporation;

NASCAR vice president Jim Hunter, who worked for Bill as both a NASCAR and ISC employee for more than 30 years and served as one of Bill's closest advisors right up until his final days;

Geri McMullin, Bill's secretary for 24 years who became in time more like a family member than an employee;

NASCAR Senior Vice President Paul Brooks, who initiated this project, and NASCAR Managing Director of Communications Ramsey Poston, who championed it;

Gary Smith, NASCAR's Managing Director of Event Logistics, who went from being Bill Jr.'s boat captain to one of his closest personal friends;

Tom Brokaw, who wrote a foreword that came from personal experience and conveyed a personal side of Bill France Jr.;

Many others throughout the NASCAR industry granted interviews and submitted anecdotes—a group that included Rusty Wallace, Ken Clapp, Humpy Wheeler, Raymond Mason, Edsel Ford, and Dick Ebersol.

And of course the heartiest thanks go to Bill France Jr., thanks that must now be offered silently in the sincere hope that somewhere, somehow, he is hearing them.

In closing, here's a true story: On a summer evening in 2005, I was leaving NASCAR's Daytona Beach offices, pulling out of the parking lot while preoccupied with a conversation I was having on my cell phone. I was probably driving slowly, but I didn't think *that* slowly.

Too damn slowly, apparently, for the guy in the Mini Cooper who zipped past me on the right into the outside lane. We both got stopped by the red light at the corner, although the sports car had arrived there a few seconds ahead of me. As I pulled up, I looked over to my right to see none other than Bill France Jr. behind the wheel. With the road clear, he made a right-hand turn and took off like a rocket. I remember thinking he must be having a blast, seeing what the little ride had.

Godspeed, Bill.

—H.A. Branham
March 2010

Introduction

On an ordinary day in the summer of 1956, I met an extraordinary man who would change my life forever. He was intriguing, with a ton of curiosity and a seemingly infinite variety of interests ranging from boats to business, from food to flying to, of course, auto racing.

He even competed himself at short tracks for a brief period prior to our wedding day—September 20, 1957. Less than two months later, on November 25, ground was broken for a new track in Daytona Beach, Florida. In what seemed like an instant, I became completely immersed in the exciting, fast-paced world of Bill France Jr.

The race was on!

After living in Winston-Salem, North Carolina, for a few months, we quickly relocated to Daytona Beach. My husband's father, Bill France Sr., had conducted a massive financial crusade, and the construction of the equally massive Daytona International Speedway was well underway.

Bill Jr. worked from dawn to dusk, 24-7, to help ensure the realization of his father's dream. In fact, the entire France family was focused on completing the project successfully. The speedway's gates indeed opened on schedule in February 1959, and I will never forget the excitement and pride we all felt. Later on, we would more fully comprehend the tremendous impact of that day as a giant step forward for our family, our community—and for racing.

In the early 1960s, our daughter, Lesa, and our son, Brian, came into our lives. They were born only 15 months apart, and we faced another challenge—parenting. Bill Jr. and I were embarking on the experience of a juggling act involving extensive travel and raising precious little children.

Bill Jr. was gone most weekends, working on the promotion of races in other states. It was a lot of work, and I always marveled at his ability to adapt and rise to every occasion.

Bill Jr. was a tough father but a good one—although his expectations were always over the top!

His best quality was his earnest love of sharing his life with others.

His legacy is his strength and determination in achieving the best and requiring the same from those around him.

He was a great friend, husband, father, and leader.

I will forever miss him.

He gave me a time to laugh, a time to cry, a time to live, a time to grow, a time for love. And in the final lap of life, he gave me a time for silence, a time for reflection, and a time for remembering the great joy of it all.

I love you, Bill.

—*Betty Jane France*

Section I

Daytona Beach
(1934–47)

Chapter One

City of Speed

As NASCAR has grown in terms of visibility and popularity, it has maintained a commitment to its roots, which were planted across the Southeastern United States in the late 1940s. A regional image developed and has persisted despite the fact that NASCAR holds races not only throughout the nation, but in Canada and Mexico, as well.

Along the way, the perception of the France family, front and center to the image, became regionalized, as well.

It's inaccurate.

While the Frances may have made their name in the Southeast, they hail from Washington, D.C.—a simple fact that is more often than not overlooked by people charting the history of what television news personality and author Tom Brokaw calls "The Greatest American Sport."

This is not to suggest a desire by the family to distance themselves from their affiliation with the Southeast. Indeed, the family still calls Daytona Beach, Florida, home. The people who run NASCAR all live only a short drive from the massive Daytona International Speedway that opened in 1959 and came to define NASCAR from a facility standpoint.

The man who came to define NASCAR left Washington, D.C., as an infant. A one-year-old Bill France Jr. was an unknowing passenger in the family Hupmobile sedan that rolled into Daytona Beach in the autumn of 1934.

To truly understand the man that toddler became, one must first understand the essence of the city where he grew up and where he worked and lived throughout his long, productive life.

His father, Bill France Sr., was at the wheel of the Hupmobile that fateful day, wife Anne was at his side—and the future was in his sights.

Hindsight and history can bring one to the conclusion that serendipity was in high gear the day the Frances arrived. Bill Sr. was an ambitious sort, a man who in time would become known for grandiose notions of success. Simply put, he dreamed big, an appropriate inclination considering he was 6'5". And in the Daytona Beach area, dreamers were welcomed.

There also was the little matter of "Big Bill" France being a big fan of the automobile. A mechanic by trade, he was intrigued by the sport of auto racing.

Make no mistake. He had landed in the right place at the right time.

Daytona Beach, still a nondescript town on Florida's East Coast in the mid-1930s, nonetheless was a town, and it owed its existence to two modes of transportation—the automobile and the railroad.

Shortly after the turn of the century, Daytona's reputation as a racing mecca already was being established. Although to be completely accurate, the community of Ormond Beach, adjacent to Daytona just to the North, was technically the true "Birthplace of Speed."

It was in Ormond, in and around what is now the intersection of State Road 40 and the coastal state highway A1A, that automobile enthusiasts from all over the world started flocking to race on the expansive, hard-packed beach and chase the land speed record. Henry Ford, Louis Chevrolet, Ransom Olds—names that became synonymous with American-made autos—were among the record-chasers. Many of the competitors stayed at the Hotel Ormond, just a short walk from the Atlantic shoreline.

The Hotel Ormond was a showplace owned by the great developer Henry Flagler, who was in the process of building a railroad system along Florida's East Coast, a system that eventually reached Key West in 1912, the culmination of what was then the ultimate dream, building a railway out and into the Atlantic Ocean to connect the string of islands known as the Florida Keys. At the turn of the century, Flagler's dream was briefly idling with his railroad stopped at Ormond Beach, making that area reachable by American industrialists and international racers.

What a magical period that was for racing and for America overall, a period that has been called the springtime of American ingenuity and industry. John D. Rockefeller, founder of Standard Oil, had a winter home called The Casements in Ormond Beach across from the Hotel Ormond. That home still stands today as a historical landmark to those memorable years. Across the street that is now four lanes and tree lined, a small gazebo at the shore of the area's intracoastal waterway, the Halifax River, is all that remains of the once-grand wooden hotel that was torn down in 1992.

And so they came to Ormond-Daytona, the speed demons and record chasers and their entourages, exploring the limitations of the internal-combustion engine and in the process laying the foundation for what would one day be Speedweeks at Daytona International Speedway.

Auto racing—the need for speed, as some might say—immediately had an attraction that was easy to understand but hard to explain. The attraction was especially strong in the Ormond/Daytona area, where the annual races came to be called the Winter Speed Carnival—now seen for what it was, the ancestor of the Daytona 500, the Great American Race.

Eventually, early in the 20th century, the quest for the land speed record moved out West to Utah and the Bonneville Salt Flats. Although those record chasers left Daytona, the area's foundation as a racing capital had been laid, and soon promoters were staging events that used both the beach and a stretch of highway bordering the beach—A1A.

One of those promoters was, of course, William Henry Getty France.

When the land speed record chasers headed west, their soon-to-be space-age technology went with them. The racing they left behind in Daytona Beach would be competition that the vast majority of Americans could truly relate to, with production-based sedans being souped up for weekend battles. Sometimes, the family car itself would be transformed into a race car.

This was auto racing for everyman, an approach Bill France Sr. understood and appreciated. The first true step Bill Sr. took toward making auto racing his business came in 1936 when the country was in the throes of the Great Depression. Daytona Beach, Florida, like much of the South, was especially suffering. Summertime temperatures approaching 100 degrees, acerbated by humidity that can best be described as hellish, served to accentuate the despair of the financially strapped.

The city of Daytona, however, had an "out" that beckoned to those astute enough to notice. Some forward-thinkers in the community recalled the not-too-distant past and became convinced that motorsports could rebound and in the process, take Daytona Beach's economy along for the ride.

Among the optimists was a man who had been there before when the sands came alive with speed, a former land speed record holder named Sig Haugdahl, who was operating a local garage. When asked for advice on a racing revival, Haugdahl conceived a plan to stage an event in 1936 that would use both the beach and a portion of State Highway A1A, the road that ran along Florida's

5

East Coast. Bill Sr. entered the race—finishing a respectable fifth in the 250-miler—and in the process he got involved in planning and promoting the event and became a partner of Haugdahl's. Much money was lost by the city—in excess of $20,000, a serious blow considering the country was waist-deep in the Depression. But Bill Sr.'s appetite had been whetted permanently, and he began promoting beach-road races himself.

Success did not come quickly, or easily.

Chapter Two

Dad

While Bill France Jr. obviously owed a portion of his existence to his father, he also owed so much of everything he became to Bill Sr.

Debts would include a list of examples set, principles followed, and ambitions fulfilled. Choosing the simplest terms to describe the growth of NASCAR and its "sister" company, International Speedway Corporation, one could say that Bill Sr. made it all possible, whereupon Bill Jr. expanded on the possibilities.

Or, try this:

Bill Sr. *created* NASCAR.

Bill Jr. *made* NASCAR.

Indeed, what a role model Bill Jr. had growing up. His earliest memories recalled a father of limitless energy and tireless work ethic. Whereas that first quality was no doubt tested by the exacting days of the Depression, the second quality was refined by those challenges. Bill France Sr. began building his fame and his family's fortune during the most unlikely of times in what most people would consider the most unlikely of places—a little-known coastal community in Northeast Florida.

"He laid the groundwork for everything I've been able to accomplish," Bill Jr. said in 2004. "You know…you can't build anything successful without a solid foundation—be it a house or a business. What my father did was make sure that NASCAR would have a solid foundation. He knew the importance of that because right from the start of this thing…. He knew we were headed toward something big. He knew that from the very beginning."

He must have. How else to explain the perseverance that outlasted the limited success of those early beach-road races?

First things first, though. Consider this an attempt to finally, permanently, dispel a portion of NASCAR lore that reappears time and again, regarding the arrival of the France family in Daytona Beach. It's not a bad story. It's just not true. The family car did not break down and in effect strand them in town. Bill France Sr. was a mechanic; he would've repaired the car and been on his way if he had so desired.

"Actually, I think Dad was on the record as telling people just that," said Bill Sr.'s younger son Jim France, now the vice chairman of NASCAR. "I think that story about the car breaking down got started by a reporter, Benny Kahn of the *Daytona Beach News-Journal.* I think Dad was originally planning on going to Miami, but there was something going on in Daytona car-related he had heard about, so he wanted to stop in town."

Bill Sr. started working at a local automobile dealership, Lloyd Buick Cadillac at 354 Beach St., facing the Halifax River on the mainland side of the city. The place is there today, although Buick is gone from the business' title. He and Annie B. found a rental house they could afford only a few miles away from the dealership and not far from the first house they would own, a bungalow-style place at 29 Goodall St. in a middle-class neighborhood tucked in between the river several blocks away and the Atlantic a mile to the East.

Bill Sr., who left the dealership in time to open a service station, renewed his on-the-fly partnership with Sig Haugdahl in 1937, following Haugdahl's inauspicious '36 event. The men had to convince the Daytona Beach Elks Club to host a second event. It did better, but not good enough for Haugdahl, who was accustomed to acclaim when it came to auto racing. In 1922, he had reached a speed of 180 mph at Daytona. He was the IMCA dirt-track champion six consecutive years from 1927–32.

Besides, Haugdahl was making a solid living operating his garage. And so he backed away from the tenuous business of promoting auto races after the '37 event.

Bill Sr., of course, soldiered on.

"When the speed-record chasers stopped coming, it left a void," Bill Jr. said. "Over the first 40 years of the 20th century, the Daytona Beach area had become synonymous with speed. So it was only natural that some community activists—like my father—would try to keep that going."

Momentum stalled, however, due to World War II. Bill Sr.'s wartime contribution was working on the construction of boats that were called "sub-chasers." When the war ended, so too did Bill Sr.'s driving career, except for the occasional "one-off" appearances. Beginning in 1946, he started concentrating on promoting events. In 1946 and '47, he oversaw a series called the National Championship Stock Car Circuit. This was the forerunner of NASCAR—only with modifieds.

Bill Sr. had become determined to blanket the sport of stock car racing with an actual organizational approach—with himself at the helm, a dictator of sorts whose benevolence would manifest itself when necessary. Such semi-absolute control was essential, he felt, in order to exact fairness from all involved—both the competitors and the promoters. He committed himself to making sure racers raced as advertised and that promoters paid those racers as promised.

"Remember…I had been racing myself, and I had put races on, too," Bill Sr. told veteran motorsports journalist Jonathan Ingram in 1983.

"There were track operators who said they'd put up a certain amount of money, and then it wouldn't be there after the race. One of the aims of NASCAR was to have a purse that would be paid when the race was over. Hospital bills weren't being paid in many cases, either. And there were small tracks all across the country with no central office keeping records of drivers' accomplishments or setting up any guidelines for the racing."

By the end of 1947, Bill Sr. was fully engaged in the founding of NASCAR.

His boy, Bill France Jr., was all of 14 years old at that point, coming of age at the precipice of history, wide-eyed at the whirlwind of activity surrounding his father, their family, and their friends in Daytona Beach, a sleepy town that was waking up and would soon be considered the world center of racing once again.

Bill France Sr. came to be known as one tough guy, a reputation his oldest son would also acquire. Along the way, though, Big Bill built many relationships that resulted in lasting loyalties. Some of those loyalties still exist nearly 20 years after his death.

Betty Faulk is loyal. The former scorer for early NASCAR great Fireball Roberts became Bill Sr.'s secretary in 1964 after several years of assisting Judy Jones, Bill Sr.'s first secretary. Faulk stayed with Bill Sr. until the late 1980s, when the advancing ravages of Alzheimer's disease ended his involvement with the business of NASCAR.

Faulk, who worked at Daytona International Speedway until 2009, remembers a Bill Sr.—who she affectionately calls, simply, "Senior"—of a different time, when he was riding shotgun on a sport that was on the move and taking advantage of the power of his planning and his sheer will.

"Senior…he was just a giant among all of us human beings," Faulk said, almost giggling, as if it was 1964 all over again. "He knew how to handle people.

He could talk people into everything, had people giving him money to build everything. He was an amazing person…but he was also, really, a very kind person.

"Senior would walk into a room and people would just do what he wanted. I once saw the Kennedys up close, and they had that same kind of charisma. It just emanated from them. Senior was that way."

"Like meetin' a mountain," recalls Faulk's good friend and longtime Daytona International Speedway employee Juanita Epton.

Faulk also describes another side of the mountain, an endearing side.

"I remember someone would come in off the street, saying something like, 'Bill, I used to buy gas from you at your service station, but I don't have any money now and I need some help.' Senior would come over to me and say. 'Go downstairs and get him $500.'

"He never forgot where he came from. He always remembered when he was poor. He struggled to get where he was. Today's generation, they don't have any knowledge of that because they never were poor."

Betty Faulk provides us a snapshot from 40-odd years ago, shedding light on a trait that Bill Sr. surely passed on to Bill Jr. Both always wore a touch of humility on their sleeves. They appreciated what they had because of their memories of when they had little. This was apparent throughout Bill Jr.'s career. He showed a special respect for the true self-made men involved in NASCAR, people like Richard Childress and Dale Earnhardt, who rose from racing short tracks to the top of the stock car world on the strength of *their* wills.

"Both of them were driven," Faulk said. "And Bill Jr. learned racing from the very ground up. If somebody had a problem, he knew because he'd been there. You couldn't put anything over on Bill Jr.…Bill Sr. either.

"Bill Sr. built the sport. Bill Jr. had to work it while it was being built.

"Bill Jr. learned everything from Senior. Senior included him in everything about the business."

Bill Sr. also included Betty Jane France in the business of NASCAR, although it was in "specialized areas." In the process, she came to know her father-in-law extremely well. She became a sidekick of sorts for Big Bill, who she recalls as "almost magical" in large part because of his imposing physical stature.

"Bill Sr.'s vision for NASCAR went beyond the race track," Betty Jane said. "He wanted to develop the social part of the sport. Bill Sr. loved parties. That's where he wanted me to help, and I did. I said 'hmmm....that's me!'

"His wife Annie B., meanwhile, wanted me to be in the bookkeeping end of things, and while I liked that, too, I didn't want that to be my sole purpose with NASCAR.

"So, while *my* Bill was busy building race tracks, I was spending time with his father. My Bill couldn't have cared less about the parties; he was definitely different from his dad in that way. Bill Jr. loved being on a tractor, loved getting in the dirt to build a track; he was like a little kid out there. You know, they were a lot alike in a lot of ways, but in their younger years, I don't think they were as much alike as later on in their lives."

Jim France said his older brother was "going to school," so to speak, on a daily basis. The subject was always the same: NASCAR 101.

"We grew up in the family business, so from a very young age, Bill was listening to Dad and to the people we might have over at the house talking business," Jim said. "Our house was kind of the office for Mom for years for a lot of things. In the early days when Bill was growing up, we had a gas station, but Dad ran all of his racing stuff, in terms of the business side, out of the house. Dad would have meetings, and Bill was hanging around, picking up on things."

In October 2004, Bill France Sr.—who died in 1992 at the age of 82—was inducted posthumously into the Automotive Hall of Fame, located in Dearborn, Michigan. Bill Jr. accepted the honor on his father's behalf and gave a speech that was heartfelt but also provided a mini history lesson to those in attendance. His respect for his father shone through.

"I know of some other father-son relationships that weren't very good, and the son couldn't do anything that the father approved of," Bill Jr. said that night. "I never had that problem. For us, it couldn't have been better from that standpoint. We had a good relationship.

"When I look back on everything we've been able to do, in many cases I guess you could say I simply followed the lead of others. Well, let me tell all of you something: There is *no one* I followed more than Bill France Sr.

"One of the things I really remember about him is how he had all these favorite sayings, which he would use from time to time, when appropriate, to make a point. Here's one of those:

On the plains of hesitation lie the bleached bones of countless millions who, when within the grasp of victory, sat and waited…and in waiting died.

"Bill Sr., as some of you who knew him remember, was not real big on waiting. He knew what he wanted for the great sport of stock car racing. He went out and made it happen and didn't wait. He would be amazed at how big NASCAR has become, but he would certainly be enjoying it, no doubt about that. He would like it, believe me. After all, he put a lot of hard work in it to get the sport started. Also, one thing I never heard him say was, 'We need to slow down. We don't want this to get too big.' No, I never heard him say that.

"I think I've tried to follow his style along the way. That being the case, I feel like I've served his memory well.

"I hope that, in the process, I've also served our sport well."

Chapter Three

Mom

Anne Bledsoe France, or "Annie B.," as she came to be known, was the matriarch of *two* families until her death at the age of 87 on January 2, 1992, only five months before Big Bill passed away. Born in Nathan's Creek, North Carolina, in 1904, she was a veritable mother hen to both the France family *and* the NASCAR family that included everyone from the most famous of competitors to the casual fan trying to scrape together the money to buy a precious grandstand ticket.

Always behind the scenes during her life, Annie B. has become even less noticeable with each passing year in historical accounts of both the founding and the growth of NASCAR. This is a gross injustice. Annie B. was integral to the success of both her husband and later her son, Bill Jr.

"While my Dad was climbing high to reach his far-out goals, Mom held the ladder," Bill Jr. said. "Dad certainly had visions and dreams. Mom, however, was his reality."

Much of that reality was based in keeping the books and balancing the budget for a growing sport, duties reflected by her titles as the first secretary and treasurer not only of NASCAR but also the International Speedway Corporation. Along the way, she also ran the ticket office at Daytona International Speedway, where for years she maintained a cash-only policy that was outdated to say the least. Her reasoning was that fans who could not afford up-front a trip to the races should not use credit to do so. The speedway likely lost a lot of ticket sales to that policy. It's also likely that from Annie B.'s viewpoint, that was a small price to pay for doing what she considered the right thing.

"Lesa, her granddaughter, talked her into finally allowing credit cards to be used for tickets," said NASCAR vice president Jim Hunter. "Annie B. didn't think the money from the Daytona 500—or any race for that matter—was NASCAR's to keep until the races had been run. So what you had was all this money and all these checks that had been paid for tickets just sitting around until the races were run. Annie wouldn't cash the checks or spend the money until the people had been given the product they'd paid for."

In recent years, NASCAR has been outspoken about wanting to reconnect with its core fans. One must surmise that Annie B. would love that. From NASCAR's earliest days, she had the core fans in mind. In addition to the credit card aversion, she always felt there should be some tickets obtainable for the working person that were available on race day. Her philosophy was to not sell all the tickets before that walk-up crowd had a chance to, well, walk up.

She was also unconvinced about the stability of corporate ticket-block sales. She worried that a corporation could always change its plans at the last minute in terms of attending guests or employees, leaving highly noticeable patches of empty seats on race day.

"She thought that selling too many corporate seats could come back to bite you," Hunter said. "Don't overload that circuit was the way she saw it."

The irony of the mindset of NASCAR's first "First Lady"—when measured against the recent economic climate that has seen many corporations pull back their financial commitments in major sports throughout the United States—cannot be ignored. NASCAR has not been immune. Anne Bledsoe France, were she around today, would likely be wagging a finger, offering a stern "told you so."

"In the last couple of years, look at what has happened," Hunter continued. "Some tracks have committed huge blocks of tickets to sponsors, and sponsors have then pulled out. Those tracks have then had huge amounts of tickets to sell that they originally weren't worried about. I would venture to say across the board, whatever NASCAR's average attendance decline has been in the last couple years, most of the decline is due to corporate sales and not individual ticket sales. I'd be willing to bet on that. Nobody is mentioning that, but I firmly believe that's a big part of the decline. All of a sudden corporations aren't renewing their tickets, and tracks are left high and dry. Annie B. always warned against just this type of thing happening.

"She really kept an eye on all the money. She was very frugal in watching that money. There's something that Bill Jr. got from her, right there, without a doubt. His mom did not believe in spending money unless you had it to spend. I think he also got his pragmatism from her, in addition to his father of course."

Annie B. likewise kept an eye on NASCAR's image, starting with the NASCAR logo. To say she ran a tight ship is a supreme understatement.

"We had no licensing at all for years because Annie didn't want anything 'out there' with NASCAR on it," said Geri McMullin, Bill Jr.'s secretary beginning in 1984. "We couldn't even give out a NASCAR decal. The only thing available to fans was a postcard at the speedway switchboard. There was no gift shop, nothing.

"Then I remember one year it was suggested that Betty Jane France design a jacket. She did, and it was a real hit. Then we got a licensing deal and some products became available through stores like Sears and JC Penney, things like kids' sleeping bags and sheets with NASCAR race cars on them. That was our first venture into licensing.

"Annie B. was very, very protective of the NASCAR mark. She didn't want it just being applied anywhere to anything. Slowly but surely, however, with Bill Jr. taking over more and more of the operation, NASCAR started working more and more on licensing, and we got the ball rolling. And Annie B. was involved in that change, too, right up until the end of her life."

In trying to explain his mother's old-school approach to finance, Jim France emphasized that his parents came out of the Depression Era. Hard times begat hard-line views for those who emerged and then started down the path of success, because no matter the promise of a venture in those days, there most certainly was worry. This sort of outlook surely contributed to the fiscal conservatism that may well have peaked when Annie B. took to stuffing money into cigar boxes until the boxes, stacked atop each other in the smallish NASCAR ticket office outside of Daytona International Speedway, overflowed. "I can remember seeing those boxes," Betty Faulk said. "Everyone used to always talk about that."

Added Jim France, "I think Mom's feeling was that fans paying in cash was a good controlling discipline that kept people from getting in trouble financially. Think about what we're seeing today with the economy. While we're not in a Depression *per se*, we're seeing the ills that easy credit can cause. Credit standards were relaxed for awhile and then people couldn't pay it off and now they're struggling. Mom came out of the Depression environment and her simplistic solution was to not encourage fans to go out on a limb but rather encourage them to pay as you go—when it came to NASCAR-related spending."

Business-like to a fault, that was Annie B. Faulk has a gem of story regarding her commitment to the task at hand.

"I was in the scorer's stand one time at Daytona," Faulk said. "Someone fell off the photo stand, right in front of our stand. It was quite a traumatic thing to watch. When I came back to the ticket office, I was telling everyone about it when Annie B. looked at me and said simply, 'Betty, when you're scoring the race, you're supposed to keep your eyes on the cars.' That was just Annie. At the speedway, she was all business. When you got her away from the speedway, she showed a real sense of humor, really funny.

"While Senior was building everything, Annie B. was really a partner in everything he did. Starting with the races on the beach and going beyond, she was his business partner, no questions about that, and she was really sharp, too. She was the type of person who would just as soon tell you if you were doing something wrong. And when she did that, she was usually right."

Sounds like Bill France Jr., some might say.

"Mom," Jim France said, "was the glue that held everything together. Dad was the promotional genius. Mom was in the background making sure all the bills got paid and also making sure that if any extra money came in, that Dad didn't piss it all away."

They still call Juanita Epton by her nickname, Lightnin'. She has worked at NASCAR since 1958, and she sold tickets to the first Daytona 500 in '59. Bill Jr. took great delight in sometimes singling her out at employee gatherings, reminding everyone else that he and Lightnin' were just about all that was left from the old days, just in case anybody had forgotten.

At the start of the 2009 NASCAR season, Lightnin' was still going strong at the age of 88, putting in eight-hour days at the ticket office, helping the speedway prepare for the 51st running of the 500. Who knows how many hours she worked alongside Annie B. for all those years? She perhaps can supply the best window into what made Annie B. tick. Some of Epton's descriptions of how Annie operated, by the way, would work for a Bill France Jr. overview, as well.

"She would listen to anyone if they had a suggestion," Epton said. "Then, a lot of times when they would be done, she'd say something like, 'We've already tried that, but thanks anyway.'

"She was a person who searched for answers. She went to the deep roots of a problem to find the best solution."

Adds Betty Jane France: "Annie was *tough*. I remember one time when I was helping out with the bookkeeping…I was out of balance by nine cents or something like that. She told me that I'd have to stay at the office until I found where that nine cents was. Nine cents! You know, today I still do my own bank statements myself, and they have to balance out right down to the penny. That's how I am—and that's from her."

An argument can be made that there is quite a bit about NASCAR that is "from" Annie B. France, starting with the pervasive work ethic so diligently personified by her boy, Bill. Jr., who came to work day after day, year after year, putting in full days long after he become one of the 500 richest men in the world.

"Bill Jr. was certainly pragmatic like she was," Betty Jane said. "Not *quite* as pragmatic as she was, though."

And certainly not as low-key. Annie B. France's legacy remains her relative invisibility within the framework of NASCAR history.

The fact that she was overlooked "was by choice," said Betty Jane. "When you're shy like she was, people don't really reach out to get to know you. And for her, that was just fine."

Lesa France Kennedy, daughter of Bill Jr. and Betty Jane, is now the chairwoman and CEO of the International Speedway Corporation. She learned the business of NASCAR first from her grandmother. Always, that meant doses of tough love and hard work courtesy of the woman she affectionately called "Gram."

"I worked for her quite awhile when I was in high school in the ticket office," Kennedy said. "She was my boss there…it was interesting. She was very accurate with everything we did. She would make you go over something and then repeat it lots of times until you got it perfect. She was a real stickler for details in that way."

After graduation from Father Lopez High School in Daytona Beach, Kennedy attended Duke University. When her college days were done, she brought her degree back to Daytona and checked whatever attitude that came with it at the door of an office she shared with her Gram. She returned from college with ideas on how to make some long-overdue changes. Eventually, she sold Annie B. on the use of credit cards and the use of computers even. That's not to imply that Annie B. ever jumped into those technological waters herself. Old school, after all, does have its limits. It certainly did in this transition period.

Duke, after all, was a long way from Daytona Beach.

"It wasn't easy," Kennedy said, smiling at the memory of those days that she now cherishes.

"Gram was a skeptic. She could be pretty negative on things until you thoroughly convinced her otherwise. And my Dad, he had a real skeptical eye, too, which I think was really helpful in keeping us from making a whole lot of huge mistakes along the way."

With both Annie B. and her son, at least one knew the battle at hand.

"They would really make you over-prove your point before they got on board," Kennedy said. "Their answer to a suggestion was usually 'no' the first go-round of a discussion. That was almost an automatic. But I think that made the people who worked for them work extra-hard to really research a subject before they presented something."

Leave it to Lightnin' to add the footnote to the saga of Annie B. France.

"I got news for you: If it wasn't for her, Daytona International Speedway wouldn't be here today," Lightnin' said. "And I don't think there's anything, business-wise, that she didn't try to make our organization go.

"Yes, Bill Sr., he had the contacts to get the right resources needed for the business. But when the resources got here, it was Annie B. [who] held on to them.

"They were not a *quinela*. They were a *perfecta*."

Which made Bill France Jr.'s own success, more or less, a sure thing.

Or at the very least, a safe bet.

Chapter Four

NASCAR's Historic Weekend

The week of December 14–17, 1947, at the Streamline Hotel in Daytona Beach was a remarkable milestone in the history of NASCAR, setting the tone and precedent for the way Bill France Sr. forever operated the stock car racing organization.

De facto, Bill France Jr.—while always his own man during his years of running NASCAR—inherited the governing approach that crystallized over the course of three days that Florida winter in a four-story building on State Road A1A across from the Atlantic Ocean, as Bill Sr. created an ambitious organization known as the National Association for Stock Car Auto Racing [NASCAR].

The meetings had a laundry list of long-term ramifications for the sport of NASCAR and eventually for Bill Jr.

Historically, though, the meetings are primarily remembered for two things: a famous photograph of the gathering and an even more famous quotation by the man in charge.

The bottom line is that things moved quickly in the days and weeks after the Streamline gathering adjourned. This contrasted to the arduous 11-year build-up that prefaced the meetings, a period during which racing and Daytona Beach were anything but synonymous.

The magical period at the onset of the 1900s had seemed at times almost mythical, while the notion that the magic of racing could be recaptured in Daytona—much less expanded into a regional or national phenomenon—was greeted with increasing skepticism in many circles, even in the face of the unyielding optimism offered up by Big Bill France.

The Streamline meetings served as the catalyst. Bill Sr., sensing as much perhaps, made sure the group he called together was photographed. Twenty-four people are in the picture, seated at a table in the Ebony Lounge on the

Streamline's top floor, working amid the litter of cigarette butts, coffee cups, and half-downed cocktails.

Bill Sr. is at the head of the table, presiding over a group representing multiple constituencies. The fact that he could summon so many is a telling testament to his powers of persuasion—and his business acumen. Bill Sr. had all bases covered. In addition to the 24 people in the slightly grainy black-and-white picture, 16 others were at the meeting.

And collectively, what a group this was. Cantankerous and contentious at times, they were first brought together by the sheer force of Bill Sr.'s personality and then won over, somewhat grudgingly, by his will.

There was Bob Richards, a businessman from Atlanta who had raced in the late 1930s and had good connections in that city. Bill Sr. knew Richard's value in opening doors for NASCAR in an area destined to become a key market in the heart of the Southeast—home to what came to be called "core fans."

There was Freddie Horton, a car owner from Providence, Rhode Island. Horton *knew* New England; his presence was indicative of Bill Sr.'s foresight and vision of NASCAR having national appeal.

Jack Peters and Ed Bruce were in attendance, representing roadster sanctioning groups from the Midwest. In addition to supplying overall input from that region of the country, they were also part of a spinoff project, as Big Bill was then kicking around the prospects of a NASCAR roadster division.

Bill Sr.'s long-time partner Alvin Hawkins, a promoter from Spartanburg, South Carolina, was on hand. Hawkins became a racing legend as the long-time promoter at Bowman Gray Stadium in Winston-Salem, North Carolina. His family remains involved at the stadium today.

Of course there was the savvy Bill Tuthill, a businessman and promoter from New Rochelle, New York, who had a knack for coming up with "hooks" to attract crowds to events, a talent that would be sorely needed as NASCAR was trying to establish itself. Tuthill ran the Streamline Hotel meetings for Bill Sr. and, not surprisingly, ended up being named NASCAR's first executive secretary.

And there were so many more, rounding out representation of the then-fragmented sport of stock car racing. Pieces of a puzzle, that's what they were, with Big Bill France trying to fit them all together on the fly.

There were drivers—Bob and Fonty Flock of Atlanta, who became two stars of NASCAR's first decade; Sam Packard of Jamestown, Rhode Island; Joe Ross of Boston; Chick DiNatale from Trenton, New Jersey; the 1946 national stock car champion Ed Samples of Atlanta, who Bill Sr. named to head up NASCAR's technical committee; the immensely popular local, Marshall Teague, who worked at Big Bill's gas station as a teenager and came away from the Streamline meetings with the title of NASCAR's first treasurer; and the Atlantans who won NASCAR's first championships, driver Red Byron and car owner Raymond Parks.

There were mechanics—Jimmy Cox of Mount Airy, North Carolina, and the superb Red Vogt out of Atlanta.

There were promoters—none more important than Joe Littlejohn of Spartanburg, South Carolina, who raced against Bill Sr. before World War II. His reputation and influence throughout the Southeast was formidable.

There were people from the Daytona Beach Chamber of Commerce—Lucky Sauer and Jimmy Roberts. Here was an early nod by Bill Sr. to the importance of politicos when it came to the running of the NASCAR business, a cognizance shared by Bill Jr. throughout his life and career.

And last but by no means least, there were journalists—Larry Roller of the International News Service; Jimmy Quisenberry of *Speed Age* magazine; and the eventual local legend Benny Kahn, who covered auto racing for years at the *Daytona Beach News-Journal* and was honored by having the old media center at Daytona International Speedway named after him.

The group of media attending, as much as any group, truly reflected the savvy of Bill France Sr. With money scarce at the start, he knew he needed the best kind of advertising there is—free advertising. And you can get that only one place— via the media. Bill Sr. consorted with and cajoled the people covering his fledgling sport, setting a standard for media awareness that Bill France Jr. continued—and a standard that is followed fervently today at NASCAR, with vice president of communications Jim Hunter, a long-time Bill Jr. disciple, leading the way.

In the photograph, Bill Sr. appears to be taking a break from his lecturing and lobbying in his unique speaking style that some remember as almost numbing. The style had substance though, give him that, because at the Streamline he was laying out some themes about stock car racing's viability that still apply today. It is significant that from the start, NASCAR was about close competition and cost containment, hence the name of a championship division Bill Sr. was pushing for, a name brilliant in its simplicity: Strictly Stock.

He had hit on a competitive concept and by the end of 1947 he was a 6'5" bulldog when it came to discussing it, having flat-out nailed the basic, *elemental* appeal of what would ultimately fuel NASCAR's growth: street cars turned into race cars. That sort of early competitive landscape for stock-car racing linked NASCAR to the automotive industry in the United States from the outset, leading to the time-honored adage, "Win on Sunday, sell on Monday," that remains in play today in the marketplace, car manufacturers' economic woes notwithstanding.

NASCAR President Mike Helton said that Bill Sr. "also wanted a circuit that the vast majority of Americans could truly relate to."

Bill Jr. said that his father "founded NASCAR on the simple idea that lots of people loved revved-up engines and fast cars as much as he did."

This is the appeal that Bill Jr. expanded upon years later, when the sponsors and marketers and public relations people began populating the garage area at race tracks throughout America. And it is the same appeal that NASCAR's third-generation leader, Brian France—Sr.'s grandson, Jr.'s son—has the company capitalizing on today.

Bill Sr. also recognized that auto racing, particularly stock car auto racing, had the ability to distinguish itself from the traditional sports the American public was more accustomed to following, because while not everyone can slam-dunk or throw a touchdown pass, *everybody* drives. This was an invaluable tool in the battle for a place in the consciousness of the nation's sports fans.

In so many ways, Bill Jr. built upon his father's vision in the process of becoming a visionary himself.

Bill Sr. outlined that vision at the Streamline with some words that have evolved into NASCAR legend. Those words cover an entire wall at NASCAR's Research and Development Center in Concord, North Carolina:

"Stock car racing has got distinct possibilities for Sunday shows and we do not know how big it can be if it's handled properly.... It can go the same way as Big Car racing (Indianapolis). I believe stock car racing can become a nationally recognized sport by having a National Point Standing. Stock car racing as we've been running it is not, in my opinion, the answer.... We must try to get track owners and promoters interested in building stock car racing up. We are all interested in one thing—that is, improving the present conditions. The answer lies in our group right here today to do it."

Bill Sr.'s group became Bill France Jr.'s group, in time.

Section *II*

NASCAR—
The Beginnings
(1948–59)

Chapter Five

The First Season

No sooner had Bill France Sr. adjourned the meeting at the Streamline Hotel, work began toward getting his new organization off and running. This would not be easy, no matter how much prior planning was involved, much less the grandiose proclamations of vision and glory that Big Bill could make sound so believable given the setting.

Hard work was ahead, but at the least it would start at home.

Daytona Beach got the honors, hosting a season-opening event on the old beach-road course. The date was February 15, 1948. Six days later, the National Association for Stock Car Auto Racing was incorporated.

Red Byron won that first event and went on to capture NASCAR's first official championship, albeit in a modified machine, which didn't exactly fit into Big Bill's vision of a competition between cars that were virtually street-legal and instantly recognizable—and more importantly, identifiable—to everyone watching the action.

A few words on Byron, a native of Talladega, Alabama: He was an interesting character and an inspiring one, as well. He had suffered a serious injury to his left leg during World War II, when his Army Air Corps bomber was shot down. His car owner, Raymond Parks, helped design an extended clutch pedal that enabled Byron to compete. The leg was withered; Byron's spirit was not. Red Byron can be seen now as Big Bill France's—and NASCAR's—first great American hero, casting the mold for people like Fireball Roberts, Richard Petty, David Pearson, and Dale Earnhardt.

After Daytona, Byron and the rest went on to compete in 51 more events, an incredible odyssey for a first-year organization. The circuit featured relatively few "stock" cars. Fields consisted mostly of modifieds. The relative sparse count of potential stock cars could be traced to the country's automobile manufacturers, who were a few laps down when it came to production—for a good reason. During the war years, factories were concentrating on machinery needed in battle. Passenger cars were back-burner projects compared to tanks and the like.

There was also a bit of a public-relations concern percolating in the background, the worry was that the average race fan might not take too kindly to seeing a spanking-new sedan going door-to-door covered with dirt and grease on a race track. All things considered, modifieds were just fine, thank you, for that inaugural season. NASCAR was indeed off and running.

Fifty-two races amounted to a daunting schedule for the sort of grassroots warriors who populated stock car racing in the late 1940s, but on the upside, only seven states were involved, five of those in the Southeast: Florida (five races, two in Daytona Beach and three in Jacksonville); Georgia (12 races); Alabama (one); North Carolina (28); Virginia (four); Pennsylvania (one); and New Jersey (one).

All these years later, one could argue that the coolest thing about the 1948 schedule was that it included Martinsville Speedway in the backwoods burg of Martinsville, Virginia. In 1948, Martinsville—which had actually opened in 1947—was a half-mile dirt track encircled by merely 750 seats. Today, the paper clip–shaped oval has 65,000 seats and two races on the NASCAR Sprint Cup Series schedule, races contested on a unique layout that also has a unique surface: primarily asphalt, there are "patches" of concrete in each corner, to enable cars to get better grip in the tight turns that are oh-so-hard on brakes over the course of 500 laps.

Martinsville has the distinction as the only remaining facility from that first season still on the premier series' lineup. It remains an indelible link to NASCAR's past—and an undeniable boon to its current competitive climate as it hosts some of the closest, most intense racing of the season, especially at its annual October race that comes in the middle of NASCAR's "playoffs"—the Chase for the NASCAR Sprint Cup. The track resides in the very heart and soul of NASCAR, a status resulting from its 62-year history running concurrently with the sanctioning body. It represents everything NASCAR was—and everything NASCAR is today.

H. Clay Earles built Martinsville and also built a relationship first with Bill France Sr. and then Bill Jr., efforts that no doubt help preserve the track's status on the premier series schedule, especially in recent years when larger markets and bigger, more modern facilities have beckoned. Media covering NASCAR annually speculate on the track's future only to see Martinsville's two races return on the NASCAR Sprint Cup schedule. Earles died in November 1999.

"Clay was very close to my mother and father, and that continued throughout the years with the entire France family," Bill Jr. said when informed of Earles' passing. "He was a huge supporter of my father and everything that he did to establish stock car racing in this country. I'll tell you what Clay Earles was: He was part of the original group of believers in NASCAR, that's what. And back then, believers were a valuable commodity."

Earles' grandson, W. Clay Campbell, has extended the track's tradition and its relationship with NASCAR. Campbell was a close personal friend of Bill Jr.— who was also a part owner of the track with his brother Jim until 2004 when the International Speedway Corporation purchased Martinsville.

"Bill Jr. and my grandfather had real similar mindsets. Bill Jr. was like an idol of mine," Campbell said. "And since our family was involved with the Frances for so many years, they were like family to us. The Frances were doing races when we were doing it all those years ago, back when it wasn't cool."

Fonty Flock, one of the soon-to-be-legendary Flock Brothers, won the first NASCAR race at Martinsville held on the afternoon of July 4, 1948, and began a long-standing NASCAR tradition of racing on either Independence Day or close to it. (For years, NASCAR held a July 4 race at Daytona International Speedway; in the 1990s, the race's date was shifted to the Saturday in July nearest the Fourth.)

And lest anyone forget, the race had a significant eighth-place finisher: Bill France Sr., who concentrated on organizing and managing the sport after that day.

Chapter Six

On The Road

Much of the history of NASCAR is simply too good to be true as far as the storytelling goes. But it is true. The first decade of NASCAR's existence is ripe with tales of another time and another place, when a sport was young and a nation was rebuilding, both bolstered by the national post-World War II optimism that pervaded the 1950s.

There were no Daytona International Speedways back then, no Talladegas, no Bristols even. Darlington Raceway in out-of-the-way Darlington, South Carolina, stood as the sole asphalt superspeedway, having opened in 1950 and commenced down the road of becoming a Southeastern mecca for stock car purists. But with the exception of that strange-looking oval constructed in the shape of an egg, NASCAR racing was still a dusty dirt-track deal where fans sitting in the grandstands had to cover their drink cups in unison with every lap, lest their liquids receive a layer of silt mixed with rubber.

After NASCAR's first season in 1948, with that outlandish schedule of 52 races, the 1949 creation of the NASCAR Strictly Stock Division came closer to embodying Bill France Sr.'s vision of competition involving vehicles only slightly removed from showroom set-ups. The 1949 schedule had eight events, including a beach-road course race in Daytona Beach, the second stop on the slate. Red Byron, now officially established as NASCAR's first star, won that race and went on to win the '49 championship, following up on his '48 title in a modified.

Moving on to 1950, there was a new name for NASCAR's premier series—the Grand National Division. Let's look at the schedule at the outset of the decade. There were 19 races on that schedule for NASCAR's third season overall. The season opened Feb. 5 on the beach-road course in Daytona Beach and ended Oct. 29 in Hillsboro, North Carolina. Darlington's debut, held on Sept. 4, was won by Johnny Mantz in a Plymouth co-owned by none other than Bill France Sr.

NASCAR GRAND NATIONAL DIVISION
1950 SCHEDULE

Race	Date	Winner
1. Daytona Beach, Fla.	Feb. 5	Harold Kite
2. Charlotte, N.C.	April 2	Tim Flock
3. Langhorne, Pa.	April 16	Curtis Turner
4. Martinsville, Va.	May 21	Curtis Turner
5. Canfield, Ohio	May 30	Bill Rexford
6. Vernon, N.Y.	June 18	Bill Blair
7. Dayton, Ohio	June 25	Jimmy Florian
8. Rochester, N.Y.	July 2	Curtis Turner
9. Charlotte, N.C.	July 23	Curtis Turner
10. Hillsboro, N.C.	Aug. 13	Fireball Roberts
11. Dayton, Ohio	Aug. 20	Dick Linder
12. Hamburg, N.Y.	Aug. 27	Dick Linder
13. Darlington, S.C.	Sept. 4	Johnny Mantz
14. Langhorne, Pa.	Sept. 17	Fonty Flock
15. North Wilkesboro, N.C.	Sept. 24	Leon Sales
16. Vernon, N.Y.	Oct. 1	Dick Linder
17. Martinsville, Va.	Oct. 15	Herb Thomas
18. Winchester, Ind.	Oct. 15	Lloyd Moore
19. Hillsboro, N.C.	Oct. 29	Lee Petty

From 19 races in 1950, the schedule expanded to 41 in '51 and peaked with a lineup of 56 events in '56. Each season had a February event at Daytona Beach.

Regarding the beach-road course, has there ever been another auto racing circuit so romanticized? But it is easy to justify, is it not? That stretch of Atlantic shoreline and adjacent asphalt of state road A1A will always have the honor of being the site of NASCAR's first race in 1948, the season-opening events in 1950 and '51, and an early-season race through 1958 before being replaced on the schedule by Daytona International Speedway and the Daytona 500 in February 1959.

The beach-road layout was the descendant of the beach-only runs of years before. It actually was a bit south of Daytona Beach, on the Northern side of the community of Ponce Inlet. The course length was 4.1 miles—lengthened from a pre-NASCAR 1930s distance of 3.2 miles. The start-finish line was on the pavement, where cars raced southward for two miles then made a hard left onto the sand, then headed north for two miles before another left-hander put them back onto AIA.

That second left-hander is now marked, perhaps fittingly, by a restaurant that is more of a bar—Racing's North Turn Beach Bar & Grille, recognized as a historic landmark in February 2007 by the Ponce Inlet Historic & Archaeological Preservation Board.

In the 1950s, Bill France Jr.—by then an ambitious, intuitive teenager—worked those races, and he liked to facetiously boast that he was "in charge of the signage."

One area of signage was classic Bill Jr.

It seemed that from the outset of the beach-road races, enterprising spectators found it somewhat simple to avoid paying the price of admission. Rather than parking along A1A and walking up to the ticket gates, they would find a spot along the Halifax River, which was/is Daytona Beach's intracoastal waterway, leave the vehicle, then trudge their way a couple yards or so toward the beach across the sand dunes, dodging the palmetto scrub.

This tactic had basically always been a problem for promoters of the beach-road races. Bill Jr. had an ingenious remedy. He had large signs made up and placed strategically in the dunes separating the river from the beach, with a clear warning:

BEWARE OF RATTLESNAKES

While contrived, in truth it wasn't that much of a stretch; palmettos always have been a haven for snakes in Florida.

Bottom line:

"It worked," Bill Jr. said.

Ticket sales reflected that pronouncement.

After Daytona, it was time to hit the road, and it was there that Bill Jr. truly learned the business of NASCAR. He learned it in places like Langhorne, Pennsylvania, and Winchester, Indiana. And North Carolina of course—Charlotte, Hillsboro, and North Wilkesboro…Weaverville and Raleigh…Hickory and Shelby… Gastonia and Salisbury.

And in Winston-Salem, where perhaps the majority of the early education of Bill France Jr. took place, working at a quarter-mile speedway within a high school football stadium, a place where you not only heard the cars but felt them as they roared around, lap after lap, week after week.

Bowman Gray Stadium still hosts NASCAR-sanctioned racing as part of the NASCAR Whelen All-American Series. From 1958–71 it was part of NASCAR's premier series, and for a time it held a popular event on the Monday after Easter. Prior to that 14-year run, NASCAR raced at the Forsyth County Fairgrounds in Winston-Salem for two races in 1955. That's now a historically insignificant prelude because of Bowman Gray's long-running success. Bowman Gray, in fact, is considered by some to be NASCAR's first true success.

For Bill Jr., it was a time where not only was a business learned but friends were made. It was a time for lots of hard work—and also a helluva lot of fun.

He, like his father, also tried his hand at racing—with mixed results. A less-than-epic evening at Bowman Gray pretty much ended the son's racing aspirations. Bill Jr. was zipping around the quarter-mile in a Nash Rambler when suddenly said Rambler was flipping violently, landing upside down on the backstretch. It looked bad.

Big Bill France, witnesses recount, literally leapt from the second row of the press box and bounded across the race track, his long legs pumping wildly. Bill Jr., making his second start in the NASCAR Short Track Division, was okay. The car was junk. That was effectively the end of Bill France Jr.'s racing career although he would in coming years enter some off-road and motorcycle events. The way Big Bill saw it, he couldn't afford for Bill Jr. to keep racing.

Besides, there was so much to do on the business end. Big Bill needed the kid's help, and wrecking cars was not helping anyone.

"In the summertime back then, Mom and Dad would move up to North Carolina to promote races in the Carolinas and Virginia," Jim France recalled. "Mom and Dad became partners with Alvin and Eloise Hawkins at Bowman Gray, which is still running today with the Hawkins family managing it. Alvin and Eloise would also come down to Florida in the winter and help Mom and Dad with the beach races. Alvin was our first flagman in Daytona.

"When Daytona International Speedway got built, Mom and Dad soon ended up spending more and more time in Florida, so they sold their interest in the stadium to Alvin and Eloise.

"When Bill was up in North Carolina, he and Joe Hawkins—Alvin and Eloise's son, who was like a brother to Bill—spent a lot of time 'bill-posting,' tacking fliers on telephone poles and barns. Hey, that was the way they promoted things back then. Instead of spending a lot of money advertising, they had to put a lot of sweat into it, putting those fliers up wherever they could."

In addition to stapling and nailing, Bill Jr. and his cohorts also used "pasters," pasting posters on metal-frame tobacco barns. Sometimes the tobacco farmers would become incensed because once those posters were pasted on, they didn't come off easily. Bill Jr. used to talk about returning to an area for the next race and pasting new posters over the old ones—whatever was left of the old ones, anyway.

Added NASCAR vice president Jim Hunter, "Hanging those posters...Bill told me he would ride through the countryside in a black-panel pickup truck with those things, which were plain old cardboard, and have to keep stopping the car, over and over, and then have to staple them to the poles."

Bill Jr. made it work though, and he had a knack for arranging his travel just right so as to arrive near the home of a good friend right around dinner time. The residences of the Wood Brothers in Stuart, Virginia, and the Petty family in Level Cross, North Carolina, were two of his favorite stops. "The only thing I liked better than Richard Petty in those days was his mama's cooking," Bill Jr. would say.

Bill-posting represented only one facet of NASCAR employment for Bill France Jr. in the 1950s. He was a madman by necessity. Bill Jr. was a starter. He was a flagman. He was a scorer. He was an inspector. He stubbed tickets at the gates. And he worked the concession stands, as well, a part of the job that lent itself to some classic stories, which he loved to tell himself.

"Those were the days when we were building stars and building facilities— plus, building a fan base," Bill Jr. said several years before his death. "In the process, we were building a sport that we knew could develop into something special. Now, they were pretty modest times to be sure. No doubt about that. But they were also great times. Memorable times...no doubt about that, either.

"I used to love going to the old Fairgrounds in Charlotte—Southern States Fairgrounds, up on the corner of North Tryon and Sugar Creek Road. The place was built way back in 1926. In the 1950s, we ran modifieds there on Friday nights. Richard Petty got his first victory there in 1960. The racing was great and so was the atmosphere.

"Anyway, I ran the concession stand at the Fairgrounds track, and that presented a few challenges, let me tell you. To start with, we didn't have any real kitchen facilities at the track, so we'd come into town and rent a room at the old

Alamo Plaza Hotel, which had rooms with kitchenettes. That's where we'd cook all of our hot dogs. Those were some great hot dogs too, guaranteed money-makers, because we had our hot-dog making down to a fine art.

"We'd cover them with chili—without beans, right out of the can—and then load them up with Tabasco sauce. We used that Tabasco sauce to sell more soft drinks. Let me tell you, if you didn't want a soft drink when you came up to the concession stand, by God, you better believe you did after taking a bite of that hot dog."

There's another good one. One hot summer evening, Bill Jr. was busy selling snow cones. They were moving that night, too. Long before the racing was done for the night, he had a problem. He ran out of snow-cone syrup. Undaunted, he kept selling—or trying to. When people came up to the concession stand and asked what flavors were available, Bill told them only one—plain. That's right, he figured he'd try and sell flavorless snow cones, ice only.

Bill Jr. also spent a bit of time as a speedway "bouncer" of sorts.

"We had the first race in what's now called the NASCAR Sprint Cup Series in June 1949 in Charlotte at the three-quarter-mile dirt track known as Charlotte Speedway off of Little Rock Road," Bill Jr. said. "That was a big day for me, for reasons that had nothing to do with the racing. My dad had this great idea that I would spend the day pulling people down off the fences to keep them from sneaking into the track without paying. I'd reach up, yank them down, then go on to the next person and do the same thing. A lot of times, I had to take off running to keep from getting my butt whipped. Because every now and then, one of the guys I pulled off the fence was a big sonofabitch who wasn't too happy with me. Keep in mind, I was only a teenager at the time."

Whenever Bill Jr. would reflect on those days of growing the sport, he would acknowledge that while the work was hard and the hours were long, that the times, while modest, were indeed fun.

"And in retrospect," he would add, "they were obviously damn important times...*damn* important. All that work we were doing was helping lay the foundation for what people are enjoying now when it comes to NASCAR."

Said Jim Hunter, "Bill Jr. learned it all from the ground up—just by being around the whole deal. The thing about him was that he was always so inquisitive. That was something he kept going with throughout all of his 74 years on this earth.

"He always wanted to know what made things work."

A footnote: Throughout the 1950s and a portion of the '60s, Bill France Jr. worked without drawing an actual salary from NASCAR. The wealth of knowledge he was accruing more than sufficed, as it put him in good stead for a boundless future.

Lightnin' Epton, NASCAR's oldest employee, knew what she was seeing in front of her own eyes, all those years ago, when Bill Jr. was learning on the fly. "Everything Bill France Jr. got when it comes to NASCAR, he earned," she said.

Chapter Seven

Betty Jane

It was 1957 and Bill France Jr., by all accounts, was cool.

Betty Jane Zachary was beautiful.

"They fell in love," said Jim France, smiling wistfully at a softer memory of his older brother, a memory he is happy to have.

Bill Jr. is gone now. Betty Jane is beautiful still.

She was, after all, a beauty queen once upon a time—1957 to be exact, at the age of 19.

"Miss Bowman Gray" was her title, and not long afterward, Bill France Jr. was her husband.

Here's how it happened.

"I was a lifeguard at the 'baby pool' at Reynolds Park in Winston Salem, North Carolina," she said. "Reynolds Park was the landlord for Bowman Gray Stadium, which was also a city-owned facility. I was very close to my immediate boss at the park, a very nice man named Ivan Bash who knew the France family.

"Ivan told me the Frances had called and asked if he knew of any young girls in the area who might be possible candidates for a beauty contest NASCAR was having at the stadium race track. Ivan told them about me. So, while it was Ivan who got me and Bill together, he told me up front, 'This Bill France Jr. guy is wild. I don't want you going out with him. But, I thought this might be a nice opportunity for you, so I told them they could come and interview you.'"

A day or so later, Bill Jr. and Joe Hawkins showed up at the pool, and soon they were signing up the striking blonde for the contest. Betty Jane, the daughter of Marler and Jane Zachary of Winston-Salem, would be a contestant in the Miss Bowman Gray contest and in turn have a chance to compete against other track beauty queens from throughout the Southeast for the title of Miss NASCAR.

The Miss NASCAR competition would be held later in the year in Daytona Beach, where in 1957 work was soon to begin on the construction of Daytona International Speedway.

"I won the Bowman Gray contest and came down to Daytona," Betty Jane said. "There were young women from all over. I met some really neat gals that week. Bill, meanwhile, took it upon himself to decide that since I was the Miss NASCAR contestant who lived closest to him—he and his family lived in Winston-Salem in the summer—he would put himself in charge of me. He made himself my personal escort.

"He was telling people—and I didn't know this—that he wasn't escorting me around because he thought I was the cutest contestant, but because he figured he'd get to know me and then he'd have somebody to go out with when he came to Winston-Salem. I was the most *convenient* one. I found out about that later on.

"Yeah, we didn't hit it off real well at first. I thought he was kind of showy. He was cool. But he thought he was cooler than I thought he was."

Jim Hunter can concur with that. "Bill was always a very confident person," Hunter said. "And I guess he got that from his dad—and his mom. Very self-assured. And as far as his appearance, well, he was a good-looking cat when he was young. Around the race track he wore those striped shirts and white pants that all the officials wore…. Yeah, Bill *was* cool in his day, no doubt."

He soon was pulling out all the stops, as he started a whirlwind courtship of Betty Jane Zachary, who was ever mindful of Ivan Bash's words of caution but found herself being won over, albeit gradually.

"When I flew down for the Miss NASCAR contest, Bill told me he was going to fly off to the West Coast of Florida in a private airplane. He wondered if I would like to be the co-pilot of the Navajo. I wanted to downplay my excitement and coyly said, 'I think I can work it into my schedule.'

"He took me to Naples, Florida, where we picked up an associate who had some business to do with Bill Sr. Yes, here we were on this big date, picking up some man. Combining pleasure and business, you know."

(Note: That man was Spike Briggs, the owner of the Detroit Tigers, who was helping out Big Bill's project of building Daytona International Speedway through his connection with Ford and its engineers.)

Later on during the visit, Bill Jr. took a significant step by taking Betty Jane to meet his mother. That first meeting wasn't the greatest, according to Betty Jane.

"What a disaster that was," Betty Jane said. "Leading up to the Miss NASCAR contest, they had all of the contestants on local television. So the night we went on, in preparation, we were assigned a make-up artist. They really put a lot on us, and I didn't care for that. You have to understand, I was a young girl from North Carolina who wore no make-up with the exception of a little lipstick.

"So here I am with all this stuff on, not even looking like myself and after the TV show, Bill decided that was the time to go meet his mother. Well, let me tell you, I was so uncomfortable meeting that lady for the first time with my very painted face. I'm sure she was hoping I was just another pretty face and not the face of her future daughter-in-law. Make-up of that magnitude was not meant to be worn outside the TV studio. I tried to carry on an intelligent conversation with grace and poise while dying inside. I couldn't wait to scrub that make-up off.

"With Bill and I, it wasn't love at first sight, but we had a connection that led to a wonderful relationship as time went by. He was very handsome, but more than that, he was very intelligent—and that appealed to me. Plus, I liked his family; they were very nice. And he liked my family. That sort of thing, of course, is important. Annie B. finally decided I was okay, and we ended up being great allies. She and Bill Sr. were great in-laws. I learned so much from both of them.

"As it ended up, we only knew each other seven months before we got married. My mother was appalled, but she still made the time to plan a beautiful Southern church wedding."

Betty Jane did not win the Miss NASCAR title, although she was a finalist. That led Big Bill France to tell people that his daughter-in-law "didn't win Miss NASCAR, but she *did* win NASCAR."

"Actually," Betty Jane said, "both Bill Sr. and my Bill picked that phrase up and would use it. They both thought it was so endearing."

Bill and Betty Jane married on September 20, 1957, at Reynolds Presbyterian Church in Winston-Salem. The church still stands today after nearly 100 years. "It's simply a beautiful place; it's where I was baptized, too," Betty Jane said.

Suffice it to say that things were moving fast for the young couple, both personally and professionally. After merely three months of marriage, they moved from Winston-Salem to Daytona Beach, a move coinciding with the start of the Daytona International Speedway project.

They moved into a small two-bedroom apartment in the heart of Daytona Beach on Grandview Avenue across from the First Presbyterian Church. "Old apartments, but they were nice," Betty Jane recalled.

The first home they owned was on South Ridgewood Avenue in Ormond Beach, just north of Daytona. That's where they stayed until the mid-1960s when they moved to the area's beachside, as it's called, on the corner of Harvard and Peninsula, where Betty Jane lovingly planted two weeping elms. "They're still in the front yard of that home," she said. "They're beautiful."

And from the beachside came the final move, to Peninsula Drive in Daytona, with a backyard bordered by the Halifax River.

"And that," said Betty Jane, "is where we lived for the next 30 years."

And during most of those 30 years, Bill France Jr. presided over the operation of NASCAR, taking over the organization's presidency from his father in 1972. Betty Jane, meanwhile, needed to find her own niche or, to use the racing parlance, "her own deal."

Which she did, comfortably growing into the role as the "First Lady of NASCAR" while at the same time being a bit uncomfortable when she had to hear herself introduced in that manner.

From her days as being NASCAR's "social point of contact," Betty Jane has evolved along with the sport, becoming immersed in various charitable causes, starting with the Junior League, then with the pediatric care units at Halifax Medical Center in Daytona Beach and Homestead Hospital in Homestead, Florida. Both units are called "Speediatrics" because of the racing-themed decors that Betty Jane France has helped design. The units are aimed at brightening a child's stay through the use of bright colors, race-car illustrations, and staff that tries to allay the trepidation and fears of young patients—and their parents and siblings.

Speediatrics has become the most visible beneficiary of the NASCAR Foundation, NASCAR's charitable arm that was formed in 2004 with Betty Jane as its visible chairperson.

"When children come to a Speediatrics facility, their care is placed in the hands of some wonderful doctors and nurses," she said. "But those children also find their way into the hearts of the people providing that care. Which is the way it should be, I think. Anyone who has visited Speediatrics—or any children's hospital ward—recognizes the importance of the work being done and the care being given.

"When children come to Speediatrics, they know they are in a place where they can feel safe and secure—at a time when they most need to feel that way. Adding to their safety and security is the simple but vital aspect of having a little fun while they are being treated. The combination of medical care and emotional care and having some fun along the way is something that sets Speediatrics apart. That combination has helped define Speediatrics."

In addition, Betty Jane immersed herself in interior design, taking classes on weekends to learn that business, a commitment that led to the opening of her own design business in the 1980s called Heather Fields.

But it is Speediatrics, in many ways, that has defined Betty Jane France, who not only won NASCAR but has also won over her own separate and unique group of admirers and supporters while operating on the sport's periphery. She complemented Bill France Jr. perfectly in every way. And now she is embellishing his legacy while working on her own.

Old Ivan Bash, it seems, had nothing to worry about after all.

Chapter Eight

Building the Tri-Oval

Bill Jr. had these khakis. Four, maybe five pairs, as Betty Jane remembers it. Dutifully she washed them and stretched them across an aluminum "stretcher" in the backyard, leaving them to dry in the hot Florida sun.

"I put them on the board, and that way I didn't have to iron them over and over," Betty Jane said. "Don't you just love that visual? I don't miss those days. I wonder if they still even have those stretchers anymore?"

Washing those khakis was not always easy. Bill Jr. did not come home clean for at least two years while he and his father were involved in the building of Daytona International Speedway on State Road 92, several miles from the beach. This project is where Bill Jr. truly began pouring his heart and soul into the business of NASCAR.

It was a project that was at once white collar and the bluest of blue collar. It was a project that yielded one of the everlasting images of Bill Jr. riding a tractor across what would eventually be a portion of the 2.5-mile tri-oval, looking back at the camera and smiling widely.

As the late *Charlotte Observer* motorsports writer David Poole reminded readers, "That photo was not staged."

Indeed, it was but a snapshot from the long hours of the hard work that Bill France Jr. loved.

"I sort of 'grew up' with the project kind of around the dinner table," Betty Jane said. "The main engineer, a man named Charles Moneypenny, and all the other people involved, were always around.

"The project wasn't a surprise. I knew they were going to do it, but I couldn't even imagine how big it was going to be.

"The whole thing now seems like a dream."

Which it was—Big Bill France's dream coming to life with his namesake at his side.

"My father knew the beach racing couldn't go on forever," Bill Jr. said in 2006, a year before his death. "He had long foreseen the day when NASCAR would be a sport with big modern race tracks, and he tried to get the speedway project started earlier than we did.

"He knew that racing on the sand was a novelty. He also knew that racing on asphalt and concrete was the future. And the way he saw it, what better place to start realizing the future than Daytona Beach? He wanted to build his business, but he also wanted his community to benefit. He went out [and] got some advice and support from local politicians and businesses on how to go about building a permanent facility. At the end of the day, Daytona International Speedway was created."

Bill Jr. turned 24 in 1957 and had been around NASCAR for 10 years, save for his two-year (1953–55) stint in the navy. After his graduation from Seabreeze High in Daytona Beach in 1951, he had briefly attended the University of Florida. His real education was still to come of course, and after a number of years of cruising the Southeast working the short tracks with his parents, he was prepared for the next level of his NASCAR learning process.

Bill Jr. wasn't the only one going to school during the construction of Daytona International Speedway. It was an unprecedented concept, and the land chosen was not exactly cooperative.

"Bill was involved in the construction from the get-go," his brother Jim France said. "I was in junior high school when they started. I came out with Dad but didn't really do anything. I'd come on the weekends, hang around, and stay out of the way basically, playing in the dirt.

"It was interesting to watch. They had a tremendous amount of dirt to move and a lot of swamp to fill in and stabilize, so we could build on top of it. It was really quite a process with the drainage, with the muck…it was a mess. I remember we had these huge bulldozers pushing the swamp muck—gumbo or whatever they called it—out of the way. And then we had problems with the soil when it rained. It would turn into something like a sponge and cars coming in and out of the infield would get stuck. We would bring in shell to stabilize the road. For years we spent thousands of dollars brining in shell and getting people unstuck. Then we finally got enough money to pave the interior roads."

While NASCAR has taken advantage of opportunities that were presented over the years, there have been other times when NASCAR created its own opportunities. The notion of constructing Daytona International Speedway was all about creation, about making something literally from nothing.

Indianapolis Motor Speedway served as a model of sorts, but it also was a target. Bill France Sr. had worked at Indy in the 1930s on a pit crew. And while he always marveled at the grandeur of the 2.5-mile oval and the Indianapolis 500, he also was puzzled somewhat by the appeal that the place—and its signature race—held for fans, because at Indianapolis, spectators are able to watch very little of the racing on any one lap due to the flatness of the oval and the vastness of the facility. Big Bill's long-term vision for NASCAR included big tracks where fans could actually see the action.

Daytona International Speedway would be different. As big as Indy—only better, with out-of-this-world banking that would create the effect of spectators looking out at a giant cereal bowl, enabling those spectators, especially the ones highest in the grandstands, to indeed see the cars all the way around the oval.

Make that the tri-oval, the name given to the "kink" in the frontstretch, an idea of Bill Sr.'s, so drivers would not feel like they were constantly turning. That also would give the new speedway even more flavor to call its own.

Whatever affinity Bill Sr. held for Indianapolis was jolted permanently in 1954, when a visit by he and Annie B. soured as they were basically thrown out of the speedway. Bill Sr. blamed not the speedway itself but rather the American Automobile Association, which sanctioned the Indianapolis 500 and had developed an adversarial relationship with NASCAR since the stock car organization came into existence. Legend has it that Bill Sr. told people that he and his wife decided they would go back to Florida and build their own damn speedway.

And from there perhaps sprang the true impetus to rival Indianapolis and try to outdo the hallowed ground of auto racing in America. The banking planned for Daytona would best Indy in two ways: the aforementioned benefit to fans' sight lines and enabling stock cars to go faster than they ever had anywhere.

After a series of financial stutter-steps that began in 1954, France pushed the envelope even for him by announcing in the summer of '57 that he would build the speedway himself, without financial partners, revenue bonds, or any other assistance—except for a number of loans he secured at various times to keep the project going.

Work began on November 25, 1957, a Monday—just three days before Thanksgiving. The challenges were daunting, starting with the mere preparation of the site, which was only one step up from a swamp.

But the foremost challenge was building the banking. Bill Jr. said that applying the asphalt was actually the easy part compared to the prep work. Talking to the noted reporter/author Bob Zeller for Zeller's *Official History of the Daytona 500*, Bill Jr. said, "What controlled the steepness of the banking was the sub-grade underneath the asphalt. When we piled dirt up there, we piled it to where you could compact the dirt and it wouldn't slide down the hill."

They piled it up as high as they could where the dirt would still stick together. That ended up being 31 degrees, with chief engineer Charles Moneypenny, the city engineer of Daytona Beach, guiding the task. Moneypenny also had to figure out how to match those steep turns with the long straightaways. He did so by utilizing an engineering approach derived from railroad expansion during the 19th century.

Early railroads with low speeds and wide-radius curves didn't require easements. As railway speeds increased to meet the demands of an advancing society and economy, it created a need for turns that could accommodate those speeds satisfied by gradual increases in curvatures. That new approach was called a transition spiral, or a track transition curve. The new race surface at Daytona demanded the use of this new approach, as no one had ever tried to build a track so highly banked.

After Bill Sr. enlisted the help of Moneypenny, he in turn got some valuable assistance from the Ford Motor Company's engineers, who had built Ford's test track in Detroit. The key input Moneypenny sought was with the transitions required to connect the steep turns to the straightaways.

The Ford test track wasn't banked anywhere near what Daytona would be, but it was able to yield meaningful data regarding the transitions. Moneypenny combined that knowledge with what he learned from the engineering required to build railroads, and he found a way to deliver for Big Bill.

Bill Jr. was one of the first people to ride around the race track. Betty Jane may actually have beaten him to it.

"I think I was the first person to ride around the track, along with Bill Sr.," she said. "We were going fast, too. It was cool but it was also scary because this was before they had the track finished. We were just riding around on the lime rock before they even put the asphalt down on top of it.

"I remember as we were riding around, Bill Sr. was saying, 'This is really going to be something one day.' Myself, I could not visualize how big the whole thing would be when it was finished—or that I would come to be an integral part of it with Bill Jr. You know how it is when you're growing up and you have older people in your family, the patriarchs and the matriarchs, you just get used to watching them and following them along. You get used to having them around. You think they're going to be around forever. But then, eventually, you have to 'get in there,' too.

"Bill Jr. worked hard to help build Daytona. Long hours. Late hours. He got home at dark every night. They worked night and day to get it done—which they did."

And never—*never*—was there any doubt that Daytona International Speedway would be completed, and then be a success, she added.

"With Bill France Sr., everything was always going to work. *It was just going to work.* That's the way it was with him."

That attribute transformed into an attitude. And it rubbed off on Bill France Jr., who was all of 25 years old when the first Daytona 500 was held on Sunday, February 22, 1959, and ended with what remains the most famous photo-finish in NASCAR history. It took three days of Bill Sr. reviewing photos and film to determine Lee Petty had nipped Johnny Beauchamp at the line.

NASCAR was now underway full-bore and flat-out, fueled by a race track that was an engineering marvel and had immediately become stock car racing's premier facility. Daytona International Speedway wasn't the "World Center of Racing," but by God it was up and open, scaring the hell out of drivers and leaving spectators shaking their heads at what they'd seen.

Bill Sr., Bill Jr., and their associates had pulled it off.

"There were a lot of skeptics back then—with good reason," Bill Jr. said. "Of the more than 400 acres at the speedway site, a good portion was swamp. In fact, you probably wouldn't be able to do a project like that today because of wetlands concerns.

"Yeah, it was a long, hard job—but we did it. And immediately, the speedway transformed NASCAR and in the process transformed the Daytona Beach community into something special.

"All those years ago, my dad spent long hours day after day, fighting the sun and the skeptics, trying to build a two-and-a-half-mile race track in the middle of what was then called nowhere. He made something out of nothing.

"The speedway's true importance, though, has nothing to do with economic impact, race victories, or things like that. It has to do with sheer inspiration. It stands as a testament to what people can do if they put their minds to it and their hearts into it."

Daytona International Speedway: A Timeline

April 1953: Bill France Sr. proposed construction of a new speedway in Daytona Beach, Florida.

August 16, 1954: Bill France Sr. signed a contract with city of Daytona Beach officials to build what would become Daytona International Speedway, "The World Center of Racing."

November 1955: Volusia County began improvements of local roads in anticipation of speedway traffic.

November 9, 1957: Bill France Sr. announced that the Daytona Beach International Speedway Corporation would build a 2.5-mile race track.

November 25, 1957: Work began on clearing the land at the proposed speedway site.

April 1958: Construction began.

February 1, 1959: First practice laps are run.

February 20, 1959: Two days before the Daytona 500, Daytona International Speedway held a 100-mile convertible race. The convertible race was immediately followed by a 100-mile race for Grand National "hardtop" cars—thus began twin qualifying races, which are today called The Gatorade Duel at Daytona.

February 22, 1959: The inaugural Daytona 500—also known as the "500-Mile International Sweepstakes" was held with hardtops and convertibles. It was the only Daytona 500 to ever run with convertibles. The finish of the caution-free inaugural Daytona 500 was too close to call, but Johnny Beauchamp went to Victory Lane and savored the celebration although the results were posted as "unofficial." Sixty-one hours later, Lee Petty was declared the winner in what appeared to be a dead heat between Petty and Beauchamp with the lapped car of Joe Weatherly making it a three-wide finish at the checkered flag. A clip of newsreel footage proved that Petty was the winner by a few feet.

July 4, 1959: The inaugural Firecracker 250—later increased to 400 miles—was held and won by local driver Glenn "Fireball" Roberts.

1961: The Daytona 200 motorcycle classic moved from the beach to a 2.0-mile road course inside Daytona International Speedway. Roger Reiman, who specialized in flat-track racing, won the inaugural Daytona 200 at DIS aboard a Harley-Davidson. His average winning speed was 69.26 mph.

August 27, 1961: Art Malone drove Bob Osecki's Hemi-powered, highly modified Indy car named the "Mad Dog IV" to a new world closed-course record speed of 181.561 mph.

February 11, 1962: The inaugural Daytona Continental, now known as the Rolex 24, was held as a three-hour race run counter-clockwise on the 3.81-mile road course. Dan Gurney, driving the No. 96 Lotus-Climax 19b S 2500 car, won the Daytona Continental, completing 82 laps and averaging 104.101 mph in what was the fastest sports car race ever run in the United States.

February 20, 1977: Janet Guthrie became the first woman driver to compete in the Daytona 500. She finished 12th.

August, 1978: Daytona International Speedway is repaved for the first time in its history. The project took several months to complete and was finished in time for the 1979 Daytona 500.

February 18, 1979: The Daytona 500 is televised live for the first time in event history by CBS Sports. On the final lap, Cale Yarborough and Donnie Allison crashed in Turn 3 while battling for the lead. Richard Petty held off Darrell Waltrip to win his sixth Daytona 500, while Yarborough and Allison began a heated debate that turned into a fist fight with Allison's brother, Bobby, jumping into the fray.

February 13, 1982: The inaugural event of NASCAR's new Busch Series (formerly the NASCAR Sportsman Division) was held with Dale Earnhardt coming home as the series' first winner.

July 4, 1984: President Ronald Reagan served as Grand Marshal for the Pepsi Firecracker 400 and gave the starting command, "Gentlemen, start your engines!" while aboard Air Force One. Reagan arrived mid-race, called the race with MRN Radio's Ned Jarrett, and witnessed Richard Petty's historic 200th NASCAR win. It was the first time in NASCAR history that a sitting president attended a race.

February 9, 1987: Dawsonville, Georgia, driver Bill Elliott set the Daytona 500 qualifying record with a speed of 210.364 mph.

July 4, 1992: President George Bush served as the Grand Marshal for the Pepsi 400. He gave the starting command for Richard Petty's final NASCAR race at Daytona International Speedway.

February 7, 1998: Dale Earnhardt became the first driver to tackle the 2.5-mile high-banked tri-oval under the newly installed lighting system in a special 20-lap test following Daytona 500 qualifying.

February 15, 1998: On his 20th attempt, Dale Earnhardt finally earned his first and only Daytona 500 victory in the 40th annual running of the Great American Race.

October 17, 1998: Jeff Gordon won the first Pepsi 400 ever run under the lights at Daytona. The Pepsi 400 was delayed until October because of the summer wildfires.

February 18, 2001: On his 463rd career Cup start, Michael Waltrip held off teammate Dale Earnhardt Jr. to win the Daytona 500, his first career victory. His owner, Dale Earnhardt, died following a last-lap crash in Turn 4.

July 7, 2001: Dale Earnhardt Jr. won the Pepsi 400, his first career DIS victory and 11 years to the day that his father won his first then-Winston Cup race at DIS.

February 15, 2004: President George W. Bush served as Grand Marshal for the Daytona 500, and Dale Earnhardt Jr. won "The Great American Race" on his fifth attempt. The race was also the first for new sponsor, Nextel.

February 18, 2007: Kevin Harvick nipped Mark Martin at the start/finish line to capture the closest Daytona 500 finish since the advent of computer scoring in 1993 with a margin of victory of .020 seconds. This finish was also the eighth closest in the NASCAR Sprint Cup Series history.

February 17, 2008: Daytona International Speedway hosted the historic 50th running of the Daytona 500 NASCAR Sprint Cup Series race. A sell-out crowd witnessed Ryan Newman make a last-lap pass of Tony Stewart to win the most anticipated event in racing history. The victory was the first Daytona 500 triumph for both Newman and his car owner, Roger Penske.

February 15, 2009: The 50th anniversary running of the Daytona 500 was won by Matt Kenseth.

Source: Daytona International Speedway

Section III

The Future Beckons
(1960–70)

Chapter Nine

Lesa

It was the spring of 1961. Bill France Jr. and Betty Jane France had themselves a little girl. Lesa Dawn France was born May 24, 1961. Fittingly, that was smack dab in the middle of one of the biggest weeks of the NASCAR season—then and now—as the World 600, now called the Coca-Cola 600, would be held four days later at Charlotte Motor Speedway.

It was one helluva week, and Lesa's parents were beside themselves with joy.

"I remember Lesa was only about five days old, and Betty Jane brought her into the office so we could all see her," said Betty Faulk, Bill Sr.'s former secretary. "Lesa was just a teeny-tiny little thing, all wrapped up in blankets. Betty Jane was so excited and so proud."

Being proud never stopped. It only accelerated.

"She was the model child," Betty Jane said. A perfect student, all straight-As all the time, and the teachers all loved her. She was the type of child anyone would just love to call their daughter. She excelled in everything—she was always into gymnastics, music, art...art is her hobby and calming force."

Betty Jane contrasts this memory to that of her son Brian, a year younger than Lesa, who was, as they say "all boy," keeping teachers on their toes at all times.

Brian is the subject of the next chapter in this work, but here's a preview of what his mother was alluding to. While in elementary school, Brian was guilty of standing on a chair and moving the classroom wall clock ahead 15 minutes so his class could go to lunch early. It apparently took the teacher a week to figure this out, whereupon an investigation ensued and led to the tallest kid in the class, the only one who could reach the clock—Brian France.

Lesa France avoided such antics, and whereas Brian clearly took after his adventurous father—remember how Betty Jane was warned that Bill Jr. was "wild"—Lesa followed her mother's demure, elegant lead.

Good grades led to a good school—Duke University.

And then came what to some people was a surprise, as Lesa brought her high-powered degree back to her hometown in 1983 and went to work in the Daytona International Speedway ticket office with her grandmother, Annie B. France.

"I never could see her doing what she's doing, and that's amazing to me," Betty Jane said. "And it was her idea. With Brian, he always knew what he was going to do, but I don't think Lesa did. We could always envision her working in a big city like New York, working in marketing or something like that."

"My parents were very open-minded about my future," Lesa said. "They gave me an opportunity, though, to work in the business."

In addition to helping her grandmother modernize the ticket operation, Lesa gradually began putting her personal stamp on the business she now heads—the International Speedway Corporation, a publicly traded company that owns and operates Daytona International Speedway, Homestead-Miami Speedway, Talladega Superspeedway, Darlington Raceway, Martinsville Speedway, Michigan International Speedway, Phoenix International Raceway, Kansas Speedway, Richmond International Raceway, Watkins Glen International, Chicagoland Speedway, and Auto Club Speedway.

Named to ISC's board of directors in 1984, Lesa was ISC's secretary from 1987–96 and the company's treasurer from 1989–96. From 1996–2003, she served as executive vice president, and she became president in 2003 when her father stepped down from that post and his dual position as NASCAR's Chairman/CEO. And in 2009, Lesa became the CEO of ISC when her uncle, Jim France, stepped down.

Several of the aforementioned race tracks have come into existence since Lesa moved into a leadership capacity, in the process securing races on the NASCAR Sprint Cup Series schedule. That group of tracks reflects the desire by both "sister" companies—privately owned NASCAR and publicly traded ISC—to expand the sport of stock car racing by moving into markets beyond the Southeast. Bill Jr. called this concept "realignment," which would be aimed at expansion into "underserved areas" of fan interest but also allowing for the elimination of races at facilities that were underperforming.

Auto Club Speedway in Fontana, California, opened for NASCAR business in 1997; Homestead-Miami joined the Cup schedule in '99; Chicagoland and Kansas followed in 2001. The importance of having events in the nation's second-largest (Los Angeles) and third-largest (Chicago) markets is considerable as

NASCAR continues its drive to become a true national sport while also staying loyal to its roots.

Lesa's work has been noticed beyond the auto racing industry; several times she has been named to the list of the country's "Top Female Sports Executives" by Street & Smith's *Sports Business Journal.* That publication selected her as "The Most Influential Woman in Sports Business" in 2005.

In addition, *AutoWeek* magazine listed her as "one of the 10 Secret People Who Will Change The World," while the *Charlotte Observer* chose her "one of the 25 most influential people in NASCAR from 2001–06."

Such honors speak volumes. But then, so do the cherished memories of a lady in her late eighties who watched Lesa grow up, then grow into her current status.

"Let me put in some good words for Lesa," said Betty Faulk, who retired from ISC in 2009. "In the old days, people would try to talk Bill France Sr. into setting up a retirement plan for his employees. Bill would turn that over to this man who worked for him and that man would say, 'If they want a retirement, they should save their money.' But after Lesa came in, we got a retirement plan.

"Something else that changed after she started working with us was how raises were handled. In the old days, people would sit in a meeting and say, 'Well, let's give this woman a raise of three percent but this other woman, she has a husband with a good job, so let's give her one percent. Things like that, you know. Well, Lesa changed things and wouldn't allow that sort of approach.

"Lesa was always so smart. And just a good girl."

ISC veteran Lightnin' Epton said that one of the happiest days in Annie B.'s life was when Lesa returned from Duke for good.

"To think that her granddaughter was going to help carry on what the family started, it just made her so happy," Epton said. "Lesa turned out to be a true France—right off the bat.

"And immediately she was one of the gang. She came in and just tackled her job. She did whatever she was supposed to do and never pulled rank on anybody."

In the spring of 1988, Lesa married Bruce Kennedy, a plastic surgeon from California. They had a son, Ben, in 1991, expectedly a bright young man. Ben called his grandfather Mr. France, even though Bill Jr.'s office wall had a framed crayon drawing by Ben of race cars placed prominently for all to see upon entering.

Several years ago, young Ben got the racing bug himself. He started driving in a short-track class called Super Trucks. Not long before Bill Jr. died in June 2007 after years of ill health, he got down to New Smyrna Speedway south of Daytona Beach and watched his grandson race. It was a good night.

It has become precious with the passage of time. On July 10, 2007, just five weeks after Bill Jr. died, Bruce Kennedy and NASCAR pilot Michael Klemm died in a small plane crash in Sanford, Florida. Kennedy was flying the plane. Three other people on the ground also died in the accident.

"I was prepared for Bill because he had been sick for so long," Betty Jane France said. "His death was inevitable. But with Bruce…I just couldn't believe it. Bruce was so important to our family. He was really our rock. But Lesa once again proved what a strong person she is, being there for all of us but particularly for Ben."

After an extended period spent out of the public eye necessitated by the tragedies, Lesa has returned and has expressed a desire to be "more out front" in her role as ISC's CEO.

Her father would be proud.

But then, he always was.

"She used to be my little girl…but now she's the president of the International Speedway Corporation," Bill Jr. told a gathering in 2004. "You feel a lot of pride as a parent when your children grow up to be fine people and then are ready to step up and keep the ball rolling, so to speak."

Chapter Ten

Brian

Brian Zachary France was born on August 2, 1962, at Halifax Hospital in Daytona Beach. He emerged from the womb and reportedly inquired about the photo-finish in the 1959 Daytona 500, demanding to know why in the hell it took his granddad three days to determine a winner.

Forgive the fiction and allow it to facetiously illustrate Brian's reputation for being remarkably inquisitive—and opinionated—about NASCAR at an early age, behavior that previewed his ascendance to NASCAR Chairman and CEO in 2003 and his growing reputation as one of professional sports' most innovative and successful executives.

Born into the unofficial title as NASCAR's prince, Brian took to his apparent birthright with a youthful zeal that was amusing but also impressive. From an early age, he had his eye on the sport that his family built. The kid, who as an adult would revolutionize NASCAR with concepts such as the Chase for the NASCAR Sprint Cup, brought ideas to the table long before it was expected by anyone.

One of his first unofficial projects was improving the massive complex known as Daytona International Speedway, recalled Betty Faulk.

"Brian was exceptionally smart. When he was young, he would come and sit in Bill Sr.'s office and talk to me," Faulk said. "He'd say, 'This is wrong, that's wrong, this thing needs to get fixed.' And he was just a kid. I'd tell him, 'Brian, you're awful smart.'

"But he'd go inside the speedway, see things he thought weren't right and I presume, would go talk it over with his father and grandfather.

"Brian was always sharp, no question about that. He was kind of a character as a little guy, and his Daddy would kind of fuss at him sometimes, but everything was always okay 'cause his Momma loved him."

His mother, Betty Jane France, laughs out loud at that tale and at the thought of her little boy in those days. She said his precociousness knew few bounds. "He'd go into his grandfather's office, sit at his chair behind that big desk, and prop his feet right up on the desk and tell people, 'I'm going to be your boss one day.' Oh yeah, he did it."

Today, Brian France blanches at the retelling of such stories, sensitive to the possibility of people thinking he had an air of entitlement as a young man. He seems visibly uncomfortable when reminded of his mischief, disbelieving that he could be so…entertaining. This is where he resembles his father the most. Something has intruded upon his no-nonsense approach to life and work, and he isn't all that happy about it.

Critiquing Daytona, he said, "was pretty presumptuous for a kid, I think. But yeah, I remember working up a long list of complaints. Bill Sr. wanted me to write them all down and give them to him. Well, I did that and when I gave him the list, he said I needed to get to work on fixing everything."

As far as the feet-on-the-desk story, "I'm hoping that was all done in a kidding fashion back then. Because, let me tell you, being here in my current position today with NASCAR, I wouldn't want a kid sitting at my desk and telling me how to run things."

Added his mother, "He pushed all the buttons. He was just full of it, too."

Brian was full of himself with a great sense of humor. Combine that with being smart as a whip, and you get the picture.

"He always knew what he wanted to do," Betty Jane said. "And boy, did he ever defy his dad."

Talk about pushing buttons. But then, Bill Jr. pushed back. One way he did that was by putting Brian to work in the maintenance area at Daytona International Speedway.

That assignment, working under the speedway's maintenance supervisor Red Pugh, proved relatively brief. Buttons were being pushed all around at the time. Long, hot Florida summer days on a lawn tractor didn't sit all that well with the young man. Since he had been given such a God-awful job, however, he figured he would make the most of it. The way Betty Jane remembers it, Brian messed up by removing the canopy atop the tractor. But he had a good reason. He had a date pending that night and wanted to look good with a nice tan.

This decision was greeted less than warmly by Bill Jr., when he drove into the infield and spotted the tractor, sans top—and sans son, who was taking a break.

Bill Jr. had not the least concern for tans. He asked Red what had happened to the tractor. Red didn't want to tell on Brian, but Bill Jr. kept pressing and finally got the low-down.

Brian France was fired on the spot.

It was only the beginning.

"I think I got fired more than any employee in the history of NASCAR," Brian said.

NASCAR vice president Jim Hunter concurred, saying, "Brian was pretty much his own person. He'd call me up and say, 'He fired me again.' I would tell him to just lay low, stay out of his dad's sight for a couple of days, and everything would blow over, which it always did."

The infamous impromptu Brian France press conference at Atlanta Motor Speedway in 1978 was another example of Brian disagreeing with his dad. This time, though, it went public with the media—big time.

The race had been over for quite awhile, and there was uncertainty about the win. Several announcements went back and forth, proclaiming first Richard Petty the winner, then Donnie Allison, then back to Petty. As night fell, NASCAR was still going through score sheets, trying to figure out things. Reporters who were waiting for the final call saw a 16-year-old kid who bore a striking resemblance to Bill France Sr. emerge from the scoring office. The kid then volunteered that he knew what had occurred, that one of the scorers had missed a completed Allison lap for two reasons: Allison passed the start-finish line on pit road that lap, and also, the scorer was too busy cheering for Petty at that crucial juncture.

Both Betty Jane and Brian's sister Lesa were at Atlanta. Jim Hunter said Lesa came running up to her mother with the news that her little brother was hosting a press conference in the garage.

Betty Jane dismissed that news. "They don't even know him," Betty Jane said.

"They do now," Lesa said.

Betty Jane loves telling this story.

"When the media found out his last name was France, well, he was in like flint," Betty Jane said. "Brian loved it, too. And Brian was right about the race finish.

"Bill Jr. was furious! But he couldn't say too much to Brian because, after all, he had it right. I remember that Bill Sr., meanwhile, thought the whole thing was great, just great."

∽

Brian France graduated from Spruce Creek High School in Port Orange, Florida, south of Daytona Beach. He attended the University of Central Florida for awhile before ascertaining he would forge on immediately in the family business.

Immediately was a relative term the way Bill France Jr. saw it.

Just as Bill Sr. had placed his son in job after job, requiring repeatedly learning processes and building of different skills sets, Bill Jr. adopted the same approach for Brian. And so, the future Chairman and CEO of NASCAR, after that nondescript stint as Red Pugh's assistant, would eventually be hired to work on NASCAR's West Coast short-track initiative, to run Tucson Raceway, and to head up NASCAR Digital Entertainment. Brian was at the forefront of establishing NASCAR's office in Los Angeles when he became the vice president for marketing.

"He also worked with the Motor Racing Network radio people for awhile, and during that time, Brian got MRN stations in Chicago and Los Angeles," Hunter said. "We had never had MRN affiliates in those two markets. As time went on, he also came to work for me on the short-track program. Bill Jr. told me not to treat him any different than anybody else. Brian did a good job.

"He's never been as interested in the technical aspects as Bill Jr. was, but on the other hand, Bill Jr. was certainly not what you would call a marketer. And Brian, for sports marketing, is as good as anyone I've ever known—anyone.

"I can remember me and Brian and Doug Fritz went to McDonald's to sell them a NASCAR sponsorship program. Back in those days, we didn't have any video capabilities for those sorts of meetings. We did a book-like presentation. It was really a face-to-face deal.

"Brian was very, very impressive presenting to McDonald's marketing people. We didn't make the sale that year, but the next year we did. Doug Fritz, now the president at Richmond International Raceway, helped Brian out for years with marketing. Fritz is one of the forgotten people in our marketing success. Brian, though, was the brains. He came up with the ideas.

58

"Going back to when Brian went to Tucson in 1989, that was, of course, Bill's idea. I was in Bill's office one day, late in the afternoon. He looked over at me and said, 'I'm sending him out there to run that track.' We had hired different managers out there, and the track wasn't doing well.

"I asked Bill why we were sending Brian out West again, at that particular time. Bill answered, 'I'll tell you why: There's nothing wrong with Brian wanting my seat. But the thing is, he wants my job *now*.'

"Brian was probably 30. He knew everything and was always arguing with his dad. But Bill was very proud of Brian. I don't know if he ever told Brian that, though. That wasn't Bill Jr.'s style. He wasn't known for handing out compliments. You were supposed to do things well; that's what you were getting paid for. That's the way he looked at it. But he also let you do your own thing if he thought you knew what you were doing. He didn't micro-manage.

"Brian…he got his feet wet in this business, that's for sure, while he was on the way up."

Bill France Jr. is gone and his children remain, two of the most powerful people in professional sports. "Things have indeed worked out as hoped," Betty Jane said.

"You want your children to do what they want to do—but Bill and I were glad they chose the family business," she said. "Family businesses have their drawbacks, but Bill Jr. planned this well, with Lesa running one company and Brian the other one. That's good because they're very different in their style of management and everything else. Also, they're siblings and they're competitive.

"Yes…. Bill Jr. did well with that plan."

Chapter Eleven

ISC

Be it a "sister" company, an affiliate, a sidebar operation, or whatever you want to call it, a publicly traded company such as the International Speedway Corporation (ISC), operating parallel—but separate—to privately owned NASCAR was always a certainty. There were several forerunners of ISC. Bill France Racing, established in 1953 by NASCAR founder Bill France Sr., was created as part of the process to start construction of Daytona International Speedway. When that massive project indeed got under way in 1957, the Daytona International Speedway Corporation came into existence. Eleven years later, during the construction of Talladega Superspeedway in Alabama, Bill Jr. changed the organization's name to ISC.

Today, ISC owns 12 major facilities that have events on the NASCAR Sprint Cup Series schedule, a group headed by Daytona. In addition, ISC also owns and operates MRN Radio, the nation's largest independent sports radio network; the Daytona 500 Experience attraction adjacent to the famous speedway's main grandstand; and Americrown Service Corporation, a provider of catering services, food and beverage concessions, and merchandise sales.

NASCAR's connection with ISC has been unwavering, with the France family at the controls of both. But ISC also has rich histories of involvement with other forms of racing, namely sports cars and motorcycles.

These twin efforts can be traced to Bill France Sr. but again, as with all things NASCAR, Bill France Jr. should get extensive, everlasting credit for taking his dad's ideas to the next level of both respectability and financial success. Sports car competition was especially important to both men throughout their careers.

In this area, however, the other son of Bill Sr. ended up taking the lead while working hand-in-hand with his older brother. Jim France emerged in time as the family member most in-tune with the "sporty cars" and cycles and in the process worked more on the ISC side of things. Today, Jim France serves as ISC's chairman of the board and keeps a careful eye on the operation of the Grand-Am Rolex Sports Car Series, which was acquired by NASCAR in 2008, and stages one of racing's biggest events, the Rolex-sponsored 24 Hours of Daytona—officially called the Rolex 24—that annually kicks off Speedweeks at the famous track, a two-week period capped by NASCAR's showcase race, the Daytona 500.

As Bill Jr. said several years ago, "People need to realize that the Daytona 500, while being the most important event in motorsports today, is still only the tip of the iceberg in terms of what goes [on] at Daytona International Speedway each and every year."

"Bill was always full-bore on the Daytona/ISC side of our businesses," Jim France said. "He shepherded those through a period of growth while he was also busy with NASCAR.

"I sort of inherited the motorcycle stuff from him when he took over NASCAR's reins from our dad, but Bill was an avid motorcyclist."

A few more words are needed here about the motorcycling element in the growth of Daytona International Speedway and ISC. While the 24-hour sports car race had helped build the race track's world-wide reputation, so too has the Daytona 200, the annual headlining event each spring that caps Bike Week. The 200 is one of the world's premier motorcycle road races and has been won by some of the sport's legends. The event started on the beach before moving to the speedway in 1961.

Bill Jr. was an avid rider and in the 1960s began competing in off-road endures. He even entered the Baja 100 once. His off-road experience led him to bring another event to Daytona for Bike Week, an annual motocross race—called "Supercross" because of the "Americanized" stadium setting. It has become a highlight of Bike Week, many years rivaling the 200 in terms of media attention and fan support. It is a motorcycle event for the casual fan, whereas the 200 attracts the purists. The Supercross course is carved from a giant mound of red clay dumped atop the speedway's infield grass. The end result is a challenging series of twists, turns, jumps, and speed bump–like ridges called "rockers."

In 2000, both Bill Jr. *and* Bill Sr. were inducted into the Motorcycle Hall of Fame, located in Pickerington, Ohio, near Columbus, mainly because of their efforts in making motorcycles a lasting part of Daytona International Speedway's schedule.

The addition of the Supercross event is another example of Bill Jr. expanding his father's concepts, this time not for the betterment of NASCAR but rather ISC. The event through the years has, like the 200, brought major stars to Daytona, including the great Bob "Hurricane" Hannah, rider-turned-Indy Car racer Jeff Ward, the mercurial Damon Bradshaw, Travis Pastrana, James Stewart, and Ricky Carmichael, who now is trying to work his way into NASCAR racing. Supercross took off in America during the 1980s and '90s; Daytona was key. For a number of years, the state of Florida hosted several events in the national Supercross schedule, with events in Orlando (Citrus Bowl) and Tampa (Tampa Stadium) joining Daytona. (The 2010 AMA Supercross schedule had both Daytona and Jacksonville listed.)

"I thought motocross was going to be a big thing," Bill Jr. said. "At first we ran the race by the lake in the back section of the speedway. My dad was the one who suggested we move the race up in front of the grandstands. After that, it really took off and started attracting big crowds."

Bill Sr. used sports cars to boost the image of the brand-new Daytona International Speedway in the early 1960s. In the process, those endeavors boosted the image of NASCAR. Bill Sr. helped form the Automobile Competition Committee of the United States (ACCUS) in the late 1950s; ACCUS became the United States' member organization in the world's preeminent auto racing governing body, the Paris-based Federation International de l'Automobile—FIA. Bill Sr. followed by taking one of NASCAR's first major stars, Fireball Roberts, over to France to drive a Ferrari in the 1958 24 Hours of Le Mans.

Bill Sr. didn't stop there. Stock car drivers disguised for several days as road racers became a routine occurrence in the 24 Hours of Daytona, which actually started out as a three-hour race in 1962 called the Daytona Continental. It's worth noting that the concept immediately attracted NASCAR types; in '62, the Ferrari-driving Roberts finished 12th in a race won by a sports car/open-wheel legend in the making named Dan Gurney.

The connection between NASCAR and sports cars moved beyond the novelty stage in 1976 as the Daytona 24 field had eight NASCAR Sprint Cup Series cars racing in their own class—Grand International. Bill Sr. lobbied Le Mans to have the same class that year. The class was added to the famed 24

Hours of Le Mans via a joint promotion between the two grand tracks. Two NASCAR teams competed at Le Mans that season.

"Dad wanted to establish Daytona *globally*," Jim France said. "He had the road course designed within the speedway when he built it. When he could afford it, he got that part of the facility operating. It was the way he wanted to position the speedway as something that could compete with Indianapolis as an international racing destination.

"That first 1962 race did just that. And we lost money on that first race. But my dad said for what we lost, he couldn't buy nearly that amount of global advertising. It was a promotional vehicle, and it turned out to be a pretty smart move. And yes, we also wanted to make it a profitable venture for the speedway, which we ended up doing."

ISC added another important sports car facility to its track lineup in 1983, purchasing an interest in Watkins Glen International in upstate New York, in a partnership with the nearby Corning Glass Company, which prefaced ISC purchasing the track outright in 1997. This marked ISC's first partnership with a Fortune 500 company.

Former Watkins Glen public relations manager J.J. O'Malley vividly remembers the interest Bill Jr. took in re-energizing the once-proud road course. O'Malley learned first-hand what many have long overlooked about Bill Jr.'s years in the motorsports business: his affinity for road racing.

"The word 'international' is in our company title, and you can't be international unless you're in road racing," said ISC president John Saunders. "Bill Jr. took that to heart."

"From a NASCAR point of view, Bill was looking at things like TV ratings and how to build the sport in that sort of way," O'Malley said. "But when he put his ISC hat on, he was all about ticket sales for the race. I can't get over the thoroughness with which he attacked tickets. He was all over it. That and credentials, too.

"He came up to the Glen in '84 and over the course of a week took a new van and literally beat it up. He drove every road there was in the vicinity of the race track. He was checking everything out in terms of security...where we needed to have ticket booths set up.... He even found himself an escape route out of the track to avoid traffic. He also found what he called a 'hot spot' over near Turn 10 where he could tell people would be able to drive up close and watch the races for free. He told us he wanted that area controlled."

This smacked of the old days so much, the days of riding around the Southeast…or putting up signs in the sand dunes warning of rattlesnakes to dissuade people from sneaking in to the Daytona "beach-road" races…or pulling would-be gate-crashers down off the fences surrounding the track in Charlotte.

This was Bill France Jr. at his best. He reveled in the behind-the-scenes nuts-and-bolts operation of a race track and even though he was, for all practical purposes, "the man," he preferred to let others in ISC be out front.

"Much of the face of ISC he put through the track presidents," said Saunders, also the former president of Watkins Glen. "But he also had a very high level of communication with track presidents. He was very much into attention to details regarding the promotion of an event, the execution of an event, even about how the tracks were talking to the media. He touched every single aspect of the ISC business because he knew it so well. He grew up in it, with him and his father building Daytona, building Talladega.

"He was definitely our leader in the boardroom and in the company overall, but again he expected the track presidents to be the leaders in their communities. He was likely to pick up the phone and call a mayor in a particular city near a race track, but he made sure the track president was talking to that mayor on a regular basis. He set expectations there, but where he really drove deep was in the fundamentals of the business. And he was tough as nails…but fair, very fair.

"You know, you're fortunate in life when you have a few people you can call your mentors. Bill was a mentor to me. He taught me this business from the ground up."

Because of that learning process, Saunders had a front-row seat to watching Lesa France Kennedy grow into her role as a leader at ISC, to the delight of her father.

"She came in with the idea of building the Daytona 500 Experience fan attraction at the speedway, and then ISC got into a track-acquisition mode and she led all of those acquisitions," Saunders said.

"Bill always kept expectations high of not only his family but everyone who worked at ISC. I know he was very proud of Lesa and our whole team."

International Speedway Corporation: A Timeline

1934   William H.G. (Bill Sr.) and Anne France move to Daytona Beach.

1947   Initial organizational meeting for NASCAR.

1948   NASCAR formally incorporated on February 21.

1953   Bill France proposes construction of a permanent speedway facility on April 4.
        Bill France Racing, Inc. becomes incorporated.

1955   Bill France Racing, Inc. changes name to Daytona International Speedway Corporation.

1957   Ground clearing for Daytona International Speedway begins on November 25.

1959   Daytona International Speedway opens. First Daytona 500 is run on February 22. Lee Petty in an Oldsmobile is declared the winner three days after the event.

1966   Bill France meets with the Talladega mayor and other city officials to propose the construction of a superspeedway on a site near Talladega, Alabama.

1968   Daytona International Speedway Corporation changes name to International Speedway Corporation.

1969   Construction on the Talladega Superspeedway begins on May 23, 1969. Talladega Superspeedway opens. Richard Brickhouse wins first Talladega 500 on September 14.

1970   Motor Racing Network goes on the air to broadcast the 1970 Daytona 500 on February 22.

1982   ISC purchases historic Darlington Raceway in South Carolina.

1983   ISC purchases interest in Watkins Glen International road course in upstate New York.

1996   ISC became 12 percent equity owner of Penske Motorsports, Inc. DAYTONA USA, "The Ultimate Motorsports Attraction," opens to the public on July 5.

1997   ISC acquires remaining interest in Watkins Glen International.
        ISC acquires Phoenix International Raceway.
        ISC announces plans to build motorsports facility in Kansas City, Kansas.

1998   ISC EVP Lesa Kennedy named one of the "Top Female Sports
Executives" by Street & Smith's *Sports Business Journal*.

ISC named to Forbes list of 200 Best Small Companies in America.

ISC joins with Indianapolis Motor Speedway and Route 66 Raceway to build motorsports facility in Chicago.

1999   Bonds sold for ISC's Kansas City project.

ISC first in motorsports to offer online ticket sales.

ISC, Trump enter into agreement to develop motorsports facility in New York area.

Daytona 500 records record television viewership.

ISC completes merger with Penske Motorsports, Inc., acquiring 4 more tracks—California Speedway, Michigan Speedway, North Carolina Speedway, and Nazareth Speedway.

The Motorsports Alliance, LLC, a limited liability company jointly owned by the Indianapolis Motor Speedway Corporation and ISC and the owners of Route 66 Raceway, LLC, announced the formation of a new company, Raceway Associates, LLC. The company plans to build a motorsports facility in the Chicago area.

ISC acquires Richmond International Raceway.

2000   Groundbreaking for Kansas Speedway in Kansas City, Kansas.

Groundbreaking for Chicagoland Speedway in Joliet, Illinois.

ISC President Jim France and ISC EVP Lesa Kennedy named to NASCAR board of directors.

ISC EVP Lesa Kennedy named one of the "Top Female Sports Executives" by Street & Smith's *Sports Business Journal*.

ISC Chairman Bill France Jr. steps down as president of NASCAR.

2001   Kansas Speedway and Chicagoland Speedway host inaugural NASCAR Sprint Cup races.

Lesa Kennedy named "2001 Top Female Sports Executives of the Year" by Street & Smith's *Sports Business Journal*.

ISC acquires remaining 10 percent of Homestead-Miami Speedway.

Bill France Jr. named "International Entrepreneur of the Year" by the University of Missouri–KC.

2003   Lesa D. Kennedy, who served as executive vice president of the company since 1996, becomes ISC president. She is the company's first female president and becomes the third-generation France to run International Speedway Corporation.

James C. France, president and chief operating officer since 1987, is named CEO.

John R. Saunders, ISC's senior vice president of operations since 1999, is named senior vice president and chief operating officer.

2004   ISC acquires Martinsville Speedway.

ISC sells North Carolina Speedway.

2007   ISC acquires remaining 62.5 percent interest in Raceway Associates LLC, owner and operator of Chicagoland Speedway and Route 66 Raceway.

William C. France passes away on June 4 and is succeeded by James C. France as chairman.

2008   The 50th running of the Daytona 500.

Groundbreaking for Daytona Live! in Daytona Beach, Florida.

2009   ISC and The Cordish Company announce plans to open a Hard Rock Hotel & Casino at Kansas Speedway by 2011 after being awarded the casino management contract for Wyandotte County, Kansas, by the Kansas Lottery Gaming Facility Review Board.

James C. France, 64, announced plans to step down from the role of chief executive officer on June 1. Mr. France will remain chairman of the board.

President Lesa France Kennedy, 47, is promoted to chief executive officer and retained her position as vice chair.

Senior vice president/COO John Saunders is promoted to president.

Chapter Twelve

A New Project: Talladega

Talladega Superspeedway serves as a 2.66-mile metaphor for a significant juncture in NASCAR's progression, a time when the old first began giving way to the new.

The race track was another pet project of Bill France Sr.'s, built 10 years after Daytona, designed to be just a little bit longer, a little bit faster—and a lot more harrowing for the drivers who dared to venture out on the high banks that were even steeper than Daytona at 33 degrees.

"Bill Sr., ever the visionary, was bound and determined to build another big track like Daytona—only bigger and better," said NASCAR vice president Jim Hunter, also the former public relations director of Talladega. "He originally looked around Spartanburg, South Carolina, but he wasn't going to get any breaks with taxes or anything else, so he went to Alabama. He knew Governor George Wallace, and the governor told Bill Sr., 'You build the track, and I'll build an interstate that will help get people in and out.' And he did.

"Bill Sr. became very well connected in Alabama, probably as good as or better connected than he was in Florida. He was always a firm believer in the political system."

The same goes for Bill France Jr., who thrived in the back-room atmosphere of local politics where deals were made—or broken. But Bill Jr.'s "belief" was balanced by a healthy dose of skepticism.

"I asked Bill Jr. one time why he was so interested in politics. He told me, 'Because you can wake up one morning and find that someone has passed a law that's put you out of business. You better stay on top of it.'"

Forty years after Talladega opened in 1969, the track has secured its place in NASCAR history, and much of that has to do with the daunting tri-oval's characteristics that first caused so much trepidation and ultimately a controversy that shook the sport to its very core. In 1987, Bobby Allison's car became airborne and nearly went through the frontstretch fencing—and into the grandstand. The sanctioning body, led by Bill Jr., responded immediately, first by mandating smaller carburetors at Talladega and Daytona, then by instituting the use of carburetor restrictor plates to limit horsepower, significantly reduce speeds, and decrease the chances of an unspeakable tragedy.

The story of that 1969 debut is one of success that came with a price. It is a story of yet another Bill Sr. dream realized, but one that may well have been a catalyst in the aging leader stepping down several years later, giving way to his ambitious son, Bill Jr.

And for Bill Jr., Talladega may have been his ultimate learning experience, the finishing touch on his NASCAR education. On this project, his duties went far beyond those he had in the construction for Daytona. He needed more than blood, sweat, and four pairs of khakis this time around.

"Talladega was really a pet project of Bill Sr.'s; he really wanted to build that track," said Bill Sr.'s secretary at the time, Betty Faulk, who remembers that the desire to make the project happen led to an increased involvement with the controversial Governor Wallace. Bill Sr. served as Wallace's campaign manager in Florida for the governor's 1972 presidential bid that ended when Wallace was shot in an assassination attempt. Wallace survived but spent the rest of his life wheelchair-bound. Betty Faulk and her daughter were recruited as Wallace delegates to the Democratic National Convention that year in Miami, where the governor spoke just months after the attempt on his life.

Talladega was built in the northern part of Talladega County. There were obstacles of course, namely in the area of financing. But the real obstacles were still to come.

In the days leading up to the first Talladega 500, at what was then called Alabama International Motor Speedway, the speeds were high, the drivers were spooked, and the tire compounds were apparently inadequate. Tire companies were unable to come up with a tire that held together very long under the unforeseen amount of stress the high-banked track was placing on the rubber. The situation resulted in a driver boycott led by Richard Petty under the auspices of a fledgling drivers' union called the Professional Drivers Association.

Bill Sr. had already dealt with a previous attempt at a union back in 1961, going so far as to ban one of the organizers, the legendary driver-partier Curtis

Turner, for life. The ban was lifted several years later, but the message remained clear that NASCAR and unions were a mix akin to oil and water.

Eight years later, Bill Sr. took the same hard line and, when faced with the possibility of the PDA boycott, he basically told the drivers not to let the track gate hit them in the ass on their way out. The boycott proceeded, putting Bill Sr. in a serious bind. Neither he nor the sport could afford a cancellation of such an awaited debut. He pieced together a field, consisting of drivers who didn't take part in the boycott, plus others from the second-tier Grand American Division that competed the day before the 500-mile event. On September 14, Richard Brickhouse won the first Talladega 500, which was halted after every 25 laps for a "competition caution" to enable teams to change tires.

The dispute served to distance Bill Sr. from the drivers in NASCAR's top series, but at the same time it enabled Bill Jr. to build relationships via a "good cop" approach.

What you had was a watershed weekend for NASCAR and the two Bills.

"Bill Jr. was right in the middle of everything at Talladega," said his brother Jim France. "There was a lot of political stuff going on in the background with the PDA. It was complex, and Talladega was the point where people decided to bring it to a head.

"I think what my brother took away from that experience was that he reached out and started getting a better working relationship with the drivers and the teams. That way going forward, if issues came up he would work *with* them. I think Richard Petty and a bunch of the guys came to have a comfort level with Bill Jr. that they didn't feel with Dad. Bill Jr. was able to really listen to the teams and drivers and then come back later with solutions that worked for everybody. Bill Jr. was able to really create good lines of communication with the teams and drivers that really helped advance the sport.

"Bill learned from that first Talladega race was that there's a better way of solving problems. I think he proactively worked to get involved with people. He listened to what people had to say. Now, those same people might not always agree with the decisions he made, but people came to respect him because he would take in everybody's input and then make decisions that were ultimately good for the sport and good for everybody who was trying to make a living in the industry."

At the end of one decade, at the dawn of a new one, the sun finally seemed to be setting on the reign of Bill France Sr., whose iron-fisted rule of NASCAR had been challenged again and for once—maybe the only time, some might say—those disputing the sport's leader appeared to have come out on top, more or less.

There were many changes on the horizon, changes in the areas of sponsorship, competition, television coverage, safety—you name it. Collectively, the challenges would demand a revised vision, a new style of leadership, so to speak, as NASCAR continued to move beyond its humble beginnings and more toward the mainstream of American sports.

In the wings, already identifying with the altered dynamics of stock car racing, stood Bill France Jr., who was starting to look more and more like a leader himself.

Section IV

Growing A Sport (1971–2000)

Chapter Thirteen

RJR and the Winston Cup

Okay, let's not mince words here: In retrospect, it's clear the partnership between the National Association for Stock Car Auto Racing and the R.J. Reynolds Tobacco Company (RJR) was a match between an outlaw sport and an outlaw product.

"A match made in heaven," said the once-devilish good ol' boy who helped broker the monumental deal, one Robert Glenn Johnson, otherwise known far and wide as "Junior."

Junior Johnson, the former moonshine runner who turns 79 this year, still enjoys telling the tale about how he sought sponsorship himself from RJR and about how that original request was dismissed by company executives as being more or less insignificant because RJR was looking for a bigger presence to help make up for the increasing limitations on advertising for tobacco products.

Big tobacco was on the ropes in the early 1970s, even though the anti-smoking movement was in its relative infancy. In April 1970, Congress enacted the Public Health Cigarette Smoking Act of 1969 which banned cigarette advertising on television and radio and required a stronger health warning on cigarette packages. Henceforth, consumers would read—if not heed—an ominous sentence on their packs: *"Warning: The Surgeon General Has Determined That Cigarette Smoking Is Dangerous to Your Health."*

RJR needed to look elsewhere to market its products. NASCAR was looking everywhere, eager for sponsor dollars to shore up its efforts at continued growth, efforts that were hampered in part by aging facilities and the simple overall cost of doing business.

Teams were feeling the money crunch, too. Junior Johnson remembers that all too well.

"What happened was RJR was advertising heavily on TV, going up against other cigarette manufacturers," Johnson said. "Around about the time the government took them off TV, I walked in and wanted to get some sponsorship from them.

"I told them I wanted $850,000 to run my car for a year. They just sorta laughed at me. So I asked them if that was too much. That's when they told me no, that they were looking for something a lot bigger. They said that with them having to come off of TV, they had $575 million that they had to do something with…I said, 'Lord have mercy, you need to go to Bill France Sr. about sponsoring NASCAR's whole deal.'

"I still thought I was going to get some money, too, but as it got down close to making the deal, RJR realized that it would be too much of a conflict of interest for them to sponsor an individual car and the series, too. So I lost out there."

RJR, of course, chose to spotlight its flagship brand, Winston, via the new NASCAR connection. The first season included sponsorship of selected events of 250 miles or longer in 1971, with those called "Winston Cup races." RJR promoted the events extensively with billboards in the vicinity of race tracks and considerable newspaper advertising. At the end of the season, top drivers in the series standings got various shares of a $100,000 bonus fund.

RJR decided to sponsor the entire season for NASCAR's top series—then called the Grand National Division—starting in 1972. The '72 schedule was pared from 48 to 31 events and thus began the unofficial but perfectly reasonable label of "modern era" in NASCAR's historical timeline.

In 1972, each race was at least 250 miles long. The aim for Winston was to make each event a major sports happening. The new name for the series had the sound of something big: the NASCAR Winston Cup Grand National Division. The NASCAR Winston Cup Series label wasn't officially applied until 1986. Winston also became the title sponsor for NASCAR's Western tour and its grassroots short-track level. The NASCAR Winston West Series operated from 1974–2003; its descendant exists still, starting the 2010 season with sponsorship from Camping World. The NASCAR Winston Racing Series ran from 1982–2001; its current incarnation is known as the NASCAR Whelen All-American Series.

Collectively, this was the most successful sponsorship in the history of motorsports with much of NASCAR's success and growth linked to Winston's involvement and the secure, almost family-like relationship between the sponsor and the sanctioning body.

That relationship, like so many other aspects of the sport, was established by Bill Sr. and embellished by Bill Jr.

"Bill Jr. did a tremendous job with Winston," Johnson said. "They helped him, and he helped them. And no way could he have done all he did without their help. It all just fell the right way…at the right time and in the right place."

Some unique individuals represented RJR through the years of its sponsorship of NASCAR, which ran for 33 years. First to the plate was the irrepressible Ralph Seagraves, who was renowned for his outlandish white-and-red outfits (the colors of Winston) and his penchant for, when seeing a race fan smoking a rival brand, immediately trading a carton of RJR smokes for the single, rival pack. Seagraves was a central figure in the initial sponsorship discussion with Johnson and NASCAR. He headed RJR's Special Events Operations department, which came to be called Sports Marketing Enterprises, from 1972–85.

Seagraves, who died in 1998 at the age of 69, was inducted into the International Motor Sports Hall of Fame in 2008, which provides an immediate indication of just how important the Winston sponsorship was to NASCAR and to the realm of sports marketing beyond stock car racing—and also just how important Winston was to the success of Bill France Jr.

"Ralph had a lot of friends because he made a lot of friends," said NASCAR vice president Jim Hunter. "He had no peer when it came to relationship building, starting with the people he worked for at R.J. Reynolds Tobacco and the people RJR worked with in motorsports. And he had his own style, to say the least. That was obvious to me the first time I met him."

Hunter had first-hand experience of Seagraves' random, man-on-the-street promotional style.

"I was down in Daytona one February, sitting in the lobby of the old Howard Johnson Hotel smoking a Kool," Hunter recalled. "In walks this guy in a garish red-and-white outfit with a cowboy hat. He asked me what I was smoking. I told him. He said he'd trade me a carton of Salems—an RJR product—for my one pack of Kools. Sounded like a good deal to me. From that day on, I smoked Salems.

"Ralph was one of the last of the good ol' boys. He was a true confidant of Bill France Sr. *and* Jr."

RJR, with Seagraves on point, went to work pouring in money to improve the facilities that hosted races that suddenly bore their branding. The first order of business in many cases, at many places, was a good paint job. Invariably, the colors used were the three Winston-themed colors—red, white, and gold. Subliminal advertising at its best immersed the NASCAR fan. There were a myriad of other improvements—in media facilities, VIP suites, and pre-race print advertising.

"Ralph Seagraves' fingerprints could be found on all of that," Hunter said. "Along the way, he eventually became a real confidant not only of the Frances but of just about everybody involved in the industry."

While Seagraves worked closely with both Bill Sr. and Bill Jr., it is probably safe to say he had more synergy with the elder France given Bill Sr.'s long-running showmanship leanings. Over-the-top promotion, to the point of being downright gaudy, did not bother NASCAR's founder.

Bill Jr. is linked historically more with the man who replaced Seagraves, T. Wayne Robertson. Seagraves mentored Robertson who, upon taking over SME, brought a more modern sensibility to the NASCAR relationship. He was the perfect man at the perfect time—as was Bill Jr.

The NASCAR relationship opened other doors for RJR. Sponsorship developed for the National Hot Rod Association (drag racing), the International Motor Sports Association (sports cars), professional golf, and professional rodeo.

The enthusiastic, engaging Robertson personified RJR's multi-faceted sports marketing initiatives until his stunning death at the age of 47 in January 1998. He and five others were killed when their duck-hunting boat collided with an oil rig just before dawn in Vermilion Parish, Louisiana.

Cliff Pennell was a RJR vice president at the time of Robertson's death; Robertson reported to him from 1996–98. After Robertson's death, Pennell replaced him at SME. Just as Robertson had altered the leadership approach handed down by Seagraves, so too did Pennell bring a different, considerably more corporate sensibility to the job. Times were changing for NASCAR at a rapid rate in the late 1990s. Pennell was another perfect fit for the sport and another perfect fit with Bill France Jr.

"I was thrown into the fire so to speak after T. Wayne's death," said Pennell, who now owns his own consulting business with NASCAR one of his main clients. "Bill Jr., Brian France, Mike Helton, Jim Hunter, and many others kind of reached out to me, and I quickly understood just what a family kind of approach NASCAR had to their business.

"Bill Jr. really did mesh well with our people, but he was one of those special people who could relate and interact with anybody. He just had that knack.

"I remember him making a comment to me one time that RJR always had the right people in the right place at the right time when it came to NASCAR.

Seagraves was just the right person to get the relationship started, Bill said. And he thought T. Wayne was the right person to take over from Ralph and move things forward. And then, Bill thought that while it was terribly unfortunate that we had to make another change the way we did because of T. Wayne's death, that the timing, as it worked out, was right for another change because of my involvement in business and the fact that I hadn't been around the sport all my life.

"You know, the RJR thing was handed off to Bill Jr. as his first major initiative that involved him with the business side of NASCAR, and he certainly, from my experience, thought the relationships we shared…that's what it was all about. But I would say there were two additional things beyond the relationship part of it. Secondly, RJR brought a more disciplined, business approach to the sport, for many years providing most of the marketing and public relations support for the sport. And third, the loyalty and commitment from NASCAR to RJR and Winston that started with Bill Jr. and permeated throughout all of the organization."

That loyalty and commitment was steadfast despite steady pressure increasingly applied to NASCAR because of the sponsorship. That pressure, Pennell said, "was unparalleled. There were limitations to what we could do in marketing, and we openly talked about those. For instance, NASCAR had a tough time marketing itself to kids because RJR and Winston obviously couldn't do that.

"NASCAR was bombarded with pressure and questions from various sources, people saying that NASCAR had outgrown RJR…that NASCAR didn't need RJR anymore…asking why NASCAR wouldn't move on, etc.

"Whenever faced with those questions or concerns, Bill Jr. would always, very passionately, respond with something like this:

'We wouldn't be where we are today if it wasn't for Winston.'

'They have a legal product.'

'We're glad to have them as our partner for as long as they choose.'"

Bill Jr. always made sure to pay all due respect—and perhaps more, some would say—to RJR and Winston whenever he had a chance to do so publicly. The foremost stage for that was always the year-end NASCAR Winston Cup Awards Ceremony that moved to the Waldorf-Astoria in New York City in 1981. The event became a showcase for stock-car racing, and Winston too, until the sponsorship ended after the 2003 season with RJR dropping out due to financial concerns.

Adds Pennell, "It says a lot about Bill Jr. that he stuck with RJR for such a long time because there were clearly many, many other companies that were not nearly as controversial standing in line ready to fill RJR's position in the sport.

"There were a lot of things we had to compromise on, some give-and-take that both parties had to work through. At the end of the day, that process was a demonstration of a true partnership."

And so it remained, the matchup of outlaw sport and outlaw sponsor, until 2003, redefining the landscape of sports marketing along the way and helping to reshape a regional pastime into a national phenomenon.

"R.J. Reynolds has been an invaluable partner for more than 30 years," Bill Jr. said in June 2003, announcing that Nextel Communications would replace Winston as the title sponsor of NASCAR's top series.

"The company and its people have invested heart and soul into our sport, helping to grow NASCAR to what it is today. We will always be grateful for our long and successful partnership."

Chapter Fourteen

Taking the Reins

The famous January 10, 1972, posed picture of Bill Sr. handing Bill Jr. a set of keys—signifying the keys to NASCAR—is a classic. On the left-hand side of the photograph is a "no smoking" sign that seems somewhat amusing since at the time, NASCAR was entering the second year of its long-term sponsorship deal with R.J. Reynolds Tobacco Company—a deal that would revolutionize not only NASCAR but the way sports marketing was viewed overall. Through the years when the photo was used, in fact, there were a number of times when the sign was cropped out of the shot. The sign, incidentally, was there for a reason—the Frances were on pit road at Daytona International Speedway, where smoking is rightfully frowned upon.

What is also amusing is to look back on the reaction within the NASCAR industry of the son replacing the father as NASCAR's president. A number of people predicted anything from disarray to disaster, resulting from NASCAR being led by a then-38-year-old man who many called Billy.

The criticism was spawned perhaps not so much by Bill Jr.'s perceived inadequacies as it was by the absolute aura Bill Sr. had constructed around himself. He had indeed become larger than life, as far as life within the world of auto racing was concerned.

The reaction to Bill Jr. taking over from his father was mixed, quite similar to what NASCAR experienced in October 2003 when Brian France was named the new chairman and CEO, becoming the company's third-generation leader.

"Goes with the territory," Brian France said.

"Generally," Jim France added, "that's kind of normal. I think it's human nature to kind of resist change somewhat or be apprehensive of change when something new is coming in."

New, though, did not mean *green*. Bill France Jr. did not lack experience.

"People didn't have the opportunity to really see what Bill was doing and learning for all those years before '72," his brother said. "He was in the background, and Dad was kind of the focal point. But Bill was involved and his understanding of everything was very deep, and whenever he had the opportunity to put his two cents in about an issue, he did so.

"I don't think it took people long to realize how smart he was and how thought-out his approach to solving problems was."

Never, his brother added, did Bill Jr. let the naysayers get to him. Just the opposite. He didn't care if people liked him. He just wanted them to like NASCAR.

"With him it was not an ego thing," Jim France said. "Naysayers did not affect him solving problems. For Bill, it was all about trying to run the business, grow it, and build the awareness of NASCAR.

"It's just that he was an unknown entity coming in."

"People absolutely did not realize how intelligent Bill Jr. was and just how much he knew about the industry," said NASCAR vice president Jim Hunter, "A lot of people overlooked the amount of time Bill Jr. had spent nurturing relationships over a period of time prior to him becoming NASCAR president. Relationships with people like the Pettys, the Wood brothers, Bud Moore, Junie Donlavey. He gained their confidence as owners. That was a big deal that paid dividends when Bill Jr. took over. He had a base of support that other people perhaps overlooked."

This was absolutely essential for Bill Jr. in the slowly subsiding wake of the 1969 Talladega controversy that some consider a catalyst in Bill Sr. stepping aside in favor of his son. Talk to people who were on the scene in those days, and you will hear opinions that when the drivers balked, Big Bill took it extremely hard.

"What happened at Talladega in 1969, with the drivers boycotting, had to take some zip out of Bill Sr.," Hunter said. "It *had* to. I mean, after everything he had done, working for years with the drivers and owners…then, after everything he'd done at Talladega, where they had the biggest advance ticket [sales] in the history of NASCAR, it had to be a tremendous letdown for him. And it might have triggered him to turn things over to Bill Jr."

The other line of thought is that the hand-off was a natural progression. At the start of the 1972 season, Bill Sr. was 62 and while his health problems had not yet surfaced, the fact of the matter was that his son was a more-robust 38 and already a veteran in the business of running stock-car races. There also was the

A young Bill France Jr. sits behind the wheel of a 1950s stock car. His racing career didn't last long.

In 1958 Bill France Jr. was right in the middle of things during the construction of the Daytona International Speedway. Many afternoons were spent on either a grader or bulldozer.

On the beach where it all began—Bill France Sr. and Bill Jr. in 1956.

Bill France Jr. was an ever-present figure on radio traffic during a race weekend at Daytona International Speedway. (1972)

Bill France Jr. in his Daytona Beach, Florida, office. (1973)

Left to right: Bill France Jr., Anne B. France, Bill France Sr., and Jim France pose for a photo at Daytona in 1973.

Bill France Jr. gets an earful in the garage area from Richard Petty (right) and Maurice Petty in 1974.

Bill Jr. (right) and his father Bill Sr. enjoy a break—and a laugh—with Chuck Pilliod, Goodyear's chairman of the board, at the race track in 1980.

Bill France Jr. and his wife, Betty Jane.

Proud papa Bill France Jr. (right) poses with his son, Brian France, and daughter, Lesa France Kennedy, in 2001.

President George Bush watched part of the 1992 Pepsi 400 from the Daytona International Speedway suites next to Bill France Jr. (right) and Betty Jane France (left).

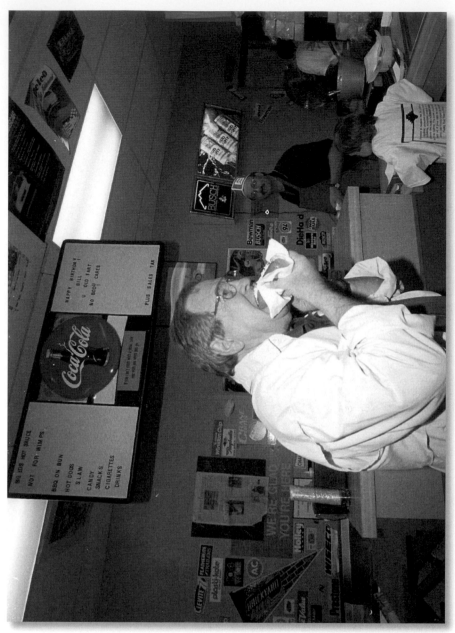

On his birthday, Bill Jr. enjoys his favorite delicacy—the hot dog.

aside that Bill Sr. would doubtless still have a hand in the day-to-day operation of the family business. The ultimate advisor to Bill Jr., as it were.

Whatever the circumstances, hindsight shows the switch was made at the right time, coinciding perfectly with so many other changes either ongoing or in the wind.

"It was a different time requiring different skills when Bill Jr. took over," Hunter said. "Something else that people overlooked was how difficult it had become to manage relationships with manufacturers because they always wanted an edge on the race track. And the manufacturers played it out in the media, complaining about the perceived differences in horsepower and aerodynamics. Bill had to manage all of that, and he did extremely well. For instance, when the manufacturers would say, 'We're going to take our bats and balls and go home' Bill would say something like, 'Well, you gotta do what you gotta do,' and in the long run it all worked out."

Veteran newspaper reporter Al Pearce's memories support Hunter's overview. Said Pearce, "I remember talking to some drivers about Bill Jr. taking over, guys like Richard Petty and Bobby Allison, and they were not nearly as worried about the transition as some people might've been. Richard Petty said, 'We watched Billy grow up. He's been around basically since Day 1. He's been right down in it all along, selling programs, doing all sorts of things. He was trained for the job all his life.'

"Richard Petty wasn't concerned at all about Bill Jr. taking over. So I figured that if Richard Petty wasn't worried, why should anybody else be worried?"

For NASCAR, 1972 was a monumental year in the sport's history. The RJR relationship was starting its second season. There was a new name for the sanctioning body's top series: NASCAR Winston Cup Grand National Division. The schedule for the series had been reduced drastically, from 48 to 31 races, in a cooperative effort between NASCAR and the new series sponsor, a move designed to focus on larger markets and better race tracks, while also making the season less arduous for the competitors, although 31 races obviously was still a lot to ask. The reduction in races also made the season more definable, enabling both media and fans to get a better grasp on a sport that was still considered largely a Southeastern-oriented niche pastime.

The schedule alteration foreshadowed the future of big-time stock car racing, a future that would inevitably leave some small towns and inadequate facilities behind.

To start in 1972, the two Daytona 500 qualifying races, then 125 miles in length, no longer counted in the series standings. That was only the start, and to all of the pundits who have so criticized NASCAR's scheduling realignment efforts of the last decade, they should consider what took place—what had to take place, really—for NASCAR to take the next step toward becoming a true, nationally recognized sport.

Gone from the schedule in 1972 were races in Macon, Georgia; Kingsport, Tennessee; Ona, West Virginia; Asheville and Hickory, North Carolina; Columbia and Greenville, South Carolina; back-to-back events in Malta and Islip, New York; South Boston, Virginia; and, in the only high-profile market exit, Houston, Texas.

This reformed landscape was being presided over by a young man who some called Billy, a name which Bill Jr., by the way, did not care for. It was a time of bridged eras. The face of NASCAR was changing, starting with the face of the man in charge.

Were there definable, watershed moments in Bill Jr.'s assumption of power? Another long-time NASCAR reporter, Ed Hinton, claims to have witnessed one in the flesh.

Hinton recounts an incident after qualifying for the 1976 Daytona 500 at Daytona International Speedway when polesitter A.J. Foyt and second-fastest qualifier Darrell Waltrip were both disqualified by the fiery NASCAR Winston Cup director at the time, Bill Gazaway. The alleged violations were nitrous oxide bottles used to supply outlandish horsepower boosts for short distances.

Up in the press box, word about the disqualifications was heard over the radio. This was going to be big news, and it sent a young Ed Hinton and several other writers scrambling down out of the speedway press box, jumping into a car, and driving through the Turn 4 tunnel into the speedway infield toward the garage area.

"This would be the first time I was around Bill Jr. a lot during a 'situation' at the track," Hinton said. "When I down got to the garage, I saw A.J. Foyt walking with his car owner, Hoss Ellington.

"Foyt was saying, 'Let's load up, let's go home.'

"Ellington was telling Foyt, 'I can't do that, A.J. I got sponsors to think about.'

"Foyt said, 'Fuck 'em, let's go home.'"

"Basically, I think Foyt was wondering whether, if he packed up and took off, NASCAR would still go ahead and run the Daytona 500 without A.J. Foyt!

"Anyway, Foyt went back into the inspection station and a few minutes later came out with Bill Jr.… Foyt had his left arm draped around Bill Jr.'s shoulders. He had a hold on him, talking. And every now and then he was pointing his finger right in Bill Jr.'s face.

"Well, throughout that whole episode, Bill France Jr. never blinked. And as far as I know, he never blinked again, either. At anything or anybody."

There is more to this story, about how Bill France Sr. showed up, parked his car in the garage with the door open and the motor running, then went and calmed Foyt down. Much has been made about the respect Foyt showed Big Bill compared to his son.

But as Hinton points out, Bill Jr. *earned* respect that afternoon, staring into the eyes of one of the toughest sonofabitches motorsports—or *any* sport—had ever seen, A.J.-frigging-Foyt.

And Bill Jr. never blinked.

"To me," Hinton said, "it felt like from that moment forward, Bill France Jr. became a stronger leader. You know, when I came in to NASCAR in 1974, I was led to believe by some of the more experienced people in the garage and in the press that Bill Jr. was not likely to be up to the task of replacing Bill Sr. over the long haul. Well, by the time he stepped down in 2003, at that point I wondered if there was anybody who could've done the job better during those years than he did.

"He grew to be a tougher and tougher individual as the job demanded. He made tough decisions. And while he may have seemed heartless toward some people at times, he was also heartless toward himself. When he chewed out a driver and told them NASCAR could get along without them, in the back of his mind, he also knew that NASCAR could get along without Bill France Jr., as well."

That was the essence of Bill France Jr. He was impressed by no one—starting with himself.

Chapter Fifteen

The Next Level

It is vital to understand that Bill France Jr. not only presided over NASCAR's ascension but in myriad ways fueled that ascension by the way he went about the everyday business of running the company. His style touched all aspects of NASCAR, having the sum effect of both expanding Big Bill France's original vision for stock car racing while also leaving that vision in the dust.

"Bill Jr.," said NASCAR president Mike Helton, "was given the reins by his father to fashion NASCAR."

The young man who had sold snowcones at short tracks, who had ridden that tractor and helped build Daytona International Speedway from the ground up, who had posted sign after sign on country roads throughout the Southeast advertising a fledgling sport, was more than equipped during the second half of his life to adjust his sensibilities to the new dynamics of a burgeoning sport.

Starting in 1972 and for the better part of three decades afterward, Bill Jr. whipped NASCAR into shape.

In terms of competition.

In terms of sponsorship.

In terms of visibility.

And in terms of popularity.

Granted, he had a lot of help, starting with the incredible support from R.J. Reynolds, which started sponsoring NASCAR's top-shelf series in 1971. But the point is, Bill Jr. maximized that help, squeezing it like a sponge, be it coming from a tobacco giant in the 1970s or his own son and an accompanying group of bright, young executives in the 1990s who were ready to nudge NASCAR onto the national map of professional sports.

By the time Bill Jr.'s tenure at the top was done, NASCAR would have races in Los Angeles, Chicago, Kansas City, Las Vegas, and Dallas-Fort Worth. And

Indianapolis, too, for God's sake. The number of races on television increased dramatically as had race purses, resulting in large part because of the increased revenue from network television. Likewise, the quality of TV broadcasts became greatly improved. Technology notwithstanding, Bill Jr. pointed to a simple reason why the shows were better—TV was paying more money to NASCAR for the rights, so they had motivation to do a better job.

"Bill Jr. took a lot of things to the next level," Jim Hunter recalled. "He knew so much. He had so much intuitive knowledge. For instance, one of the things Bill instilled in us when we were dealing with potential sponsors was the need to really study a company to understand what it might want to gain from a relationship with NASCAR. Get this: He wanted us to try and get copies of their marketing strategy plans so we could pick out our strengths within the context of those plans, finding common denominators that could seal a deal, so to speak."

Upon assuming NASCAR's leadership, Bill had immediate incoming equity with various team owners. This was a base that the new president safeguarded throughout the rest of his life.

"Bill Jr. *always* looked after the car owners because he knew the owners had to have money to keep going," Hunter said. "They had to have sponsors. During his time as NASCAR's leader, the price of running a NASCAR team escalated dramatically. You had to have pretty serious sponsors. The days of being backed by Joe's Esso station on the corner were gone. The days of getting free tires from someone were also gone. Sponsors became paramount. Bill Jr. spent a lot time helping owners find sponsors."

Jim France remembers his brother as the consummate multi-tasker on a national scale. "He was a real hands-on manager," he said. "When he took over from Dad, he went to all the Winston Cup Series races. At that time, what's now the Nationwide Series (originally Late Model Sportsman) had fallen on hard times, and he got me and Jim Hunter working to get it rejuvenated.

"And, working with Winston, Bill started the national championship for weekly racing. There were a lot of things always going on under Bill's management. And aside from the Winston Cup Series, he put just as much effort into things like getting the Nationwide Series going strong again or starting the weekly program.

The weekly short tracks were a particularly spotlighted sidebar. "After all," Jim France said, "the short tracks was where he had grown up, helping Mom and Dad during the summers in North Carolina."

A common denominator emerges repeatedly when you talk to people about the years that Bill France Jr. ran NASCAR. That denominator flies in the face of the general perception of Bill Jr. as a no-holds-barred take-no-prisoners hard-ass leader. Indeed, when a decision was made, Bill Jr. was unyielding. But he almost invariably came to a decision only after considerable input from a variety of sources.

And this is one area where he definitely separated himself from Big Bill France.

"Bill Jr., he would listen to you; Bill Sr. would not," said Bill Jr.'s longtime friend, fishing buddy, and confidante, car owner Felix Sabates.

One of NASCAR's most successful owners, Rick Hendrick, echoes that sentiment.

"Bill Jr. had a keen sense of trying to keep things even in the sport," Hendrick said. "He accommodated the manufacturers as far as he could, but at the end of the day, he would always say, 'We gotta put on a good show.' He wasn't going to alter his plans to do that because of pressure from someone.

"He had a sense of what the sport needed to succeed, and NASCAR just took off because of that. He had a sense for what the fans liked, what the competitors required, and a great sense of how to organize it all. It was like he was building on a foundation that he and his dad had talked about a lot.

"Bill Jr. knew where he wanted to take NASCAR."

The decision-making process at NASCAR was consistently criticized for years for being agonizingly slow. The slowness was by design. "It was because Bill Jr. wanted to think everything through, which would serve NASCAR better, ultimately," Hunter said.

By no means did Bill France Jr.'s time at the top of NASCAR proceed without opposition. He had his enemies.

Upon assuming the NASCAR presidency from his father, Bill Jr. inherited a rivalry that his father had dealt with for years in the form of the imposing—and often outrageous—head of Speedway Motorsports Incorporated, O. Bruton Smith.

Smith had crossed Bill Sr. back in the 1960s when he and the flamboyant driver Curtis Turner got involved with the Teamsters while building Charlotte

Motor Speedway and tried to unionize the drivers. Bill France Sr. nixed that move and threw Turner out of NASCAR for several years. The bad blood between Smith and the Frances ran deep for years afterward, understandably so.

"I can remember Bill Jr. talking to me about Bruton," Jim Hunter said. "He would say, 'Hunter, he is a *bad* person—period. His word isn't worth anything, and for that reason, I don't talk to him.'

"And for a long time Bill didn't talk to Bruton at all because Bruton would go out and say Bill said things that Bill didn't say. When Bruton tried to unionize the drivers back then, Bill Sr. was still the guru, but Bill Jr. was around and he knew what was going on.

"That was the thing about Bill Jr.—he always knew what was going on. One of his favorite things to say was when he'd sit you down, look you straight in the eye and ask, 'Okay, what's going on? What do I need to know about?'"

Smith, who declined to be interviewed for this book, is now the chairman and CEO at Charlotte-based SMI, a company that owns eight race tracks that are part of NASCAR's national series schedules. The awarding of race dates has been an inevitable source of disputes, with Smith's SMI interests at times contrasting with those of the International Speedway Corporation.

Smith's on-again, off-again feud with NASCAR may have peaked in 2004. That year, a lawsuit alleging antitrust violations filed against NASCAR and ISC by SMI shareholder Francis Ferko resulted in a settlement that awarded SMI's Texas Motor Speedway a second NASCAR Sprint Cup race date. While the suit was filed by a private individual, it seemed to symbolize the sometimes contentious relationship between Smith and the Frances. Much of that contentiousness has abated, however, since Brian France took over as chairman and CEO of NASCAR in 2003, partly because of Brian's personal relationship with Bruton Smith's son Marcus, the president at SMI's showcase track—Charlotte Motor Speedway in Concord, North Carolina.

"I think the issue Bill Jr. probably had with Bruton was that Bruton has a natural tendency to put his self-interest ahead of others," Jim France said. "That can be a successful trait sometimes in business. But when you're running a sanctioning body where you have to balance numerous interests, that won't work for long. My brother's approach was to try to understand where everybody's interests lay and then to make decisions in everybody's best interests. My sense was—and I might be totally wrong on this—that my brother did not think Bruton had that trait or ability.

"I don't think their relationship was what you'd call heated. I think they always dealt with each other in a businesslike manner. They didn't get into shouting matches."

While Bruton Smith was perhaps the No. 1 adversary for Bill Sr. and Bill Jr. in the NASCAR industry, their most-zealous critic, when you consider the body of work, had to be the legendary mechanic/crew chief Henry "Smokey" Yunick, also a long-time Daytona Beach resident who died in 2001 at the age of 77, leaving a legacy of mechanical inventiveness and nearly 30 years of confrontation with the Frances.

Yunick was the consummate wrench-turner—and arguably the greatest cheater in the history of stock-car racing or at the very least, the best there ever was at *circumventing* the rules. That proved a tough combination for NASCAR officials. Yunick had a habit of showing up to events with cars that had no chance of passing inspection and then grabbing the media's attention when those cars failed. That irritated NASCAR because everyone knew Yunick was far too skilled to think he could get cars that were way out of line through the inspection.

"I view Smokey as one of the great self-promoters, and there's nothing wrong with that," Jim France said. "He promoted Smokey Yunick."

Yunick's disagreements with Bill France Sr. got so heated that in 1970 Yunick quit fielding NASCAR entries. So when Bill Jr. took over as NASCAR's president two years later, he again inherited a situation of sorts. Hatred by proxy is the best way to describe it. Yunick's disenchantment with NASCAR and the family who ran it were detailed in Yunick's rambling, 1,100-page three-volume memoir titled, *Best Damn Garage In Town: The World According To Smokey*.

"There were probably other people who irritated my brother, but he didn't dwell on things, be it Bruton, Smokey, or whatever," Jim France said. "He was too busy trying to run the business."

Part and parcel to NASCAR's nationwide expansion has been a long-time commitment to having a viable presence on the West Coast.

"Sea to shining sea is what Bill France Sr. called it," said Ken Clapp, the former director of the NASCAR Winston West Series who remains to this day a coastal ambassador of sorts for NASCAR throughout California, making periodic visits to media outlets to preach the sport's gospel.

There has been much publicity in recent years regarding the viability of NASCAR Sprint Cup Series races at tough-sell Auto Club Speedway in

Fontana, California. The media has latched on to the storyline and consistently overlooked the main reason for NASCAR's commitment to the Golden State, which goes beyond the obvious goal of gaining attention in the nation's second-largest market, Los Angeles.

The reason is history. NASCAR had a bond with California long before it had a Los Angeles office.

Consider:

From 1970–81, the NASCAR Sprint Cup season opened not with "The Great American Race," the Daytona 500, but rather in the Golden State at the old Riverside International Raceway road course.

From 1981–86, Riverside hosted the season finale.

From 1974–80, Ontario Motor Speedway hosted the finale.

In 1979, Richard Petty clinched the last of his seven NASCAR Sprint Cup Series championships at Ontario by finishing fifth in the *L.A. Times* 500.

And that's only a small part of the story.

Back in 1951 NASCAR's fourth year of existence, there were three California dirt tracks on the schedule—Carrell Speedway in Gardena, Marchbanks Speedway in Hanford, and Oakland Stadium.

In recent years, there have been several seasons in which more NASCAR Sprint Cup drivers were from California than any other state. Jimmie Johnson, Jeff Gordon, and Robby Gordon are all Californians.

The list goes on and on, serving as an explanation for NASCAR today having three Sprint Cup events in California—two at Auto Club Speedway and one at Infineon Raceway's road course in Sonoma.

As soon as Bill France Sr. realized the NASCAR organization was going to come together back in the late 1940s, Clapp said, California was destined to play a part.

As was Clapp, who jettisoned a variety of small business interests prior to joining NASCAR and eventually took over the successful West Series.

He also became a close personal friend of Bill France Jr. as they made sure the "sea to shining sea" concept would not only survive but flourish as NASCAR's popularity took off.

When you start assessing various highlights in Bill France Jr.'s journey to take NASCAR to the next level, you cannot avoid a discussion of the Indianapolis

Motor Speedway. The pushes into mega-markets like Los Angeles and Chicago notwithstanding, Indianapolis was viewed by some as the pinnacle that would never be reached.

Prior to the epic running of the inaugural Brickyard 400 in 1994, Indianapolis Motor Speedway had long beckoned to NASCAR, increasingly so as the years passed and the ill will harbored from 1954—when Bill France Sr. and his wife were basically thrown out of the speedway—dissipated. NASCAR actually established an Indy presence in 1982 when the new NASCAR Busch Series (now the Nationwide Series) raced at nearby Indianapolis Raceway Park (IRP), west of the big track in the burg of Clermont, Indiana.

IRP (now called O'Reilly Raceway Park) had a general manager named Bob Daniels who eagerly worked with NASCAR to create a Busch Series show at the quaint, .686-mile oval. A year after the first Brickyard 400 was run, NASCAR added another event at IRP in the first NASCAR Craftsman Truck Series (now Camping World Truck Series) season.

Now there's a yearly mid-summer spectacular for NASCAR in Indy: Trucks on Friday night, Nationwide on Saturday night, and the Sprint Cup Series Sunday at IMS.

"What Bob did at IRP opened the door to what would become one of the biggest weeks in American motorsports each year," Bill Jr. said some years back.

When that door opened, Bill Jr. didn't exactly rush in; it took some time to make NASCAR Sprint Cup racing at IMS a reality. The first Brickyard 400 was long-awaited, and it delivered with a victory by a new star, Jeff Gordon, a California native who grew up in Indiana and dreamed of racing at the famed speedway.

And so the 400 has remained as a yearly highlight—a 2008 tire-wear debacle notwithstanding. NASCAR coming to Indy most certainly stands as a significant part of the Bill Jr. legacy. The Brickyard 400 coincided with the demise of open-wheel racing in the United States, that demise resulting directly from a chasm in the sport that ended with the former Championship Auto Racing Teams (CART) series competing against the new Indy Racing League founded by former IMS CEO Tony George in 1996.

With the Indianapolis 500 obviously on the IRL schedule, that led to a watered-down field for the historic race and waning interest for both open-wheel bodies. Concurrently, NASCAR was on the rise.

Between 1993 and 2002, there was an incredible shift in household television viewership for the Indianapolis 500 vs. one of NASCAR's major races, the Coca-Cola 600 held in Charlotte, North Carolina, on the same day as the 500—the Sunday before Memorial Day. In 1993, Indy's viewership was 81 percent greater than the 600. In 2002, the 600 for the first time had a larger TV audience than the 500, a six percent advantage. Thus, an 87 percent viewership shift occurred over a 10-year period.

When open-wheel racing's popularity began to fade, the appearance of stock cars and the huge crowds they attracted each summer was more than welcomed at Indianapolis Motor Speedway.

What went around had come around, indeed. The speedway that once gave the boot to Bill Jr.'s parents was now a big-time financial beneficiary of NASCAR's burgeoning popularity. Reciprocity: NASCAR had entered hallowed ground and won over countless new fans.

"I have many memories of Bill France Jr. that I will carry with me always," George said. "I had a great deal of respect for the direct approach he took to business. He understood more than most that it takes the efforts of many working together to achieve ultimate success. That is something that he learned along the way, no doubt from his father Bill Sr.

"NASCAR was Bill Jr.'s family and his business, and he woke up everyday and worked at making it better than the day before. He was very much focused on growing NASCAR's popularity and, in particular, its top series, which is how our relationship came about. His belief was that the series and championship came first and that individual races only combined to add more importance to the championship. I enjoyed the opportunity to know him and work with him to bring NASCAR's top series to Indianapolis in 1994, and I enjoyed working with him to achieve his goals."

Junior Johnson admits it now and admits it readily. He wasn't always a big fan of Bill France Jr.

Johnson, like virtually all the old-timers who were actually older than Bill Jr., calls him "Billy." "Originally, I never had any idea that Billy would one day be running NASCAR," Johnson said. "And when that came about and he finally started doing it well, it took me a long time to swallow it, to tell you the God's honest truth.

"It was just an opinion I had. I thought he can't do it...he doesn't have the charisma...he can't stand up to the people in the sport...the sport will be ruined. Well, as time went along, he proved me not 100 percent wrong but 1,000 percent wrong. I was thinking it would never happen. And when it came down to making big decisions, I don't know of one that he missed, not one. I can't think of any leader of a major corporation who has done a better job.

"People were thinking he was gonna be behind his father [as a leader]. He was so far ahead of his father, in terms of technology, reaching out to everyone. It was amazing to see him take the sport to the next level, just amazing.

"Now, me and Billy, we did fight all the time...a lot of times I was right, other times he was right. I'd admit my mistakes but he wouldn't admit to his. I'd have to say he was a sore loser in that category.

"I'd also have to say...he was one of my best friends."

Hell, even old Smokey Yunick changed his tune eventually in the late 1990s, at least as much as his predisposition toward Bill Jr. would allow.

"I'm gonna tell you right up front that the last I knew of Bill France Jr., he would've had to go through fourth grade for three more years to get an idiot's license," Yunick said. "What happened, though, is that Bill France Jr. is controlling a billion-dollar business very successfully. So apparently since I left [NASCAR], Bill France Jr., he got educated."

Seriously, Smokey said that.

Hear it for yourself. It's on YouTube.

Chapter Sixteen

Days of Thunder

In the grand scheme of all things NASCAR, the 1990 film *Days of Thunder* is insignificant to say the least. But it is nonetheless interesting to look back and see how the production played out in such a cooperative effort between Paramount Pictures and NASCAR, to the point where there were actually "movie cars" entered in NASCAR Sprint Cup Series (then Winston Cup) races, including the 1990 Daytona 500 by noted owner Rick Hendrick.

This was the ultimate promotional tool, downright revolutionary at the time—and not universally accepted in the NASCAR garage area, starting with the top driver of the day, then three-time champion Dale Earnhardt, who grumbled to the press, "We're trying to run a race," when the topic of filming actual competition was broached in interviews.

The movie was a project of co-producers Don Simpson and Jerry Bruckheimer, then riding a wave of success from the film *Top Gun* starring Tom Cruise, also the star of *Days of Thunder*, who played a young driver named Cole Trickle—a supposed amalgam name-wise of Cale Yarborough and Dick Trickle, but in terms of the character, he was patterned loosely after the mercurial Tim Richmond, a former open-wheel star who took NASCAR by storm in the 1980s, driving for Rick Hendrick's organization. (Richmond lived as fast as he drove and died due to AIDS complications in 1989. Cruise's character stopped short of mirroring Richmond's controversial personal life.)

While arguably the best movie ever made about NASCAR, it was critically panned, mainly because of the overly gratuitous use of crash footage and the over-exaggerated scenes of drivers purposely bumping and banging during competition. Cruise provided the impetus for the movie. In the late 1980s, he and fellow actor Paul Newman—who was also an accomplished sports car racer during his long life—were hanging with Hendrick at Daytona International

Speedway, taking a few practice laps around the tri-oval. Word is, Cruise was hooked, telling Hendrick, "I'm going to make a film about NASCAR," upon climbing out of a late model Hendrick had provided for the day.

In addition to the Trickle-Richmond connection in *Days of Thunder*, other characters reminded viewers of real-life NASCAR types. Randy Quaid's Tim Daland was more-or-less a cinematic version of Hendrick as Trickle's car owner. Michael Rooker's Rowdy Burns seemed to channel the intensity and on-track ruthlessness of Earnhardt. And then there was the show-stealer, Robert Duvall, portraying a crew chief named Harry Hogge, obviously a fictional version of the great Harry Hyde.

As far as Bill France Jr. was concerned, though, there was another show-stealer—Fred Thompson, playing the head of NASCAR, an imposing figure known as Big John.

"Thompson was playing me in that movie," Bill Jr. said more than once. He was proud of it, probably because the scene where Thompson stood out was remarkably true to a real-life situation that Bill Jr. had orchestrated.

In the movie, Thompson calls a mandatory meeting involving drivers Trickle and Burns and their car owners after a series of on-track dust-ups that were endangering them and their fellow competitors. The meeting is held in a hospital, where their latest wreck had sent the two drivers. Big John informs the drivers that no more wrecking will be allowed, or else they will be parked and that the sport of NASCAR would go on, just fine, without them.

In the real world of NASCAR racing, Bill France Jr. had called drivers Geoff Bodine and Dale Earnhardt to NASCAR headquarters in Daytona Beach in 1989 along with their owners, Hendrick and Richard Childress. Bodine and Earnhardt had repeated incidents during races—a public feud at 200 mph.

Bill Jr. had seen enough. He had determined he would make things right. In doing so, he would create one of the most talked-about tales in NASCAR history. The real-life meeting made Bill France Jr. larger than life.

Just like in the movies.

"I told the screenwriter, Robert Towne, the whole story about that meeting," Hendrick said, explaining how Hollywood got it right for a change.

"Earnhardt and Bodine had been wrecking each other a lot. Richard and I would talk to them about it, but then they'd get out on the track and tear each other up. One day I was talking to Bill Jr. and he said, 'This stuff has gone on long enough.'

"So about three days later, I got a call from Bill Jr., telling me to get Bodine and come down to Daytona because we needed to have a meeting. When we showed up down there, we went into the NASCAR board room—me and Bodine, Richard and Dale—and Bill Jr., who started going right around the table."

The one-sided discussion was to the point, with Bill Jr. posing hypothetical situations to the four individuals regarding their potential futures *without* NASCAR.

Hendrick's memories of the lecture are clear:

"Bill Jr. told Bodine, 'I guess you could go back home to New York and go back to racing Modifieds, or whatever.'

"He told Richard, 'You've made a pretty good living at this, so I suppose you could find something different to do.'

"He told me that I could go sell cars.'

"Then he got to Earnhardt, and he told Dale, 'I don't know what you could do. Go work on a farm or something, I guess.'

"Then he added, 'I'll tell you what's *not* going to happen: you two monkeys ain't going to fuck up my show. This thing will be here long after all of us are gone. Now, we can sit down and I can show you tapes of the races and we can talk about who was doing what to who. I don't give a damn about all that. I'm just telling you from this day forward, when you two get close to each other on the race track, there had better be a car between you, because if you so much as touch each other, I'm going to have to park you. And I'm also going to have to come down from the tower—I hope the track has a tunnel or else it'll have to be after the race—because I will have to inspect those cars, because I'll know there has to be something wrong with them for you guys to have touched on the race track. Do I make myself clear?'

"Well, we all said 'Yessir, yessir,' and then Bill said, 'Fine, now we're going to go eat.'

"He told Bodine and Earnhardt to ride together in one car, and me and Richard to ride with him. Earnhardt said he couldn't go eat because he had plans. Bill pointed him toward a nearby phone and told him, 'Change your plans.'

"Then we all went out to dinner, and that was the end of it."

Just like in the movies.

"I know Bill really enjoyed being involved in the movie," said NASCAR vice president Jim Hunter, "although he might not have been totally pleased with the way it turned out."

There's a great footnote to the *Days of Thunder* filming that says a lot about Bill Jr.'s sense of humor.

In the Daytona Beach area in early 1990, when word got out that Tom Cruise was in town shooting a movie about NASCAR, fans were always out looking for him. As a result, when Cruise and Co. traveled, they did so with a police escort.

"It got to be a joke with all the fanfare," recalled ESPN analyst Dr. Jerry Punch, who worked as a consultant on the movie. "Every time a siren went off, you thought, 'Oh, that must be Tom Cruise.'

"One time, we needed Bill France Jr. to come to a dinner with the key people making the movie. Well, Bill had seen Tom's escorts all throughout the shooting. He arranged for the speedway security people to bring him to the dinner in a long caravan with sirens blaring.

"Bill's thinking was, 'This is my show. If you guys are going to do it, I'm going to do it, too.'"

Chapter Seventeen

Japan

NASCAR's three postseason exhibition races in Japan from 1996–98—and the 1999 NASCAR Winston West Series finale in Japan—were ambitious events, the culmination of an exploration by Bill France Jr. to gauge the viability of racing stock cars outside the North American continent. Sadly, for many who were closely involved, the epic project conjures up only bad memories.

At the first of the three races in November 1996, longtime NASCAR pace-car driver Elmo Langley died after suffering a heart attack while driving around the Suzuka Circuitland oval in Suzuka, Japan, several days before the actual race. Langley was a beloved member of the NASCAR community and also part of an especially close-knit fraternity—NASCAR officials.

The very next year, Bill France Jr., en route to the return Suzuka event, suffered a serious heart attack shortly after arriving in the city of Narita. It was the beginning of the end for NASCAR's main man, an indicator that more health problems were on the way.

NASCAR's global aspirations had a previous peak in 1988 with an exhibition race in Melbourne, Australia. The Japan initiative went further with Paul Brooks, now NASCAR's senior vice president, heading it up as a young, very green "manager of special projects"—a title he basically asked for upon being handed the Japanese assignment by Bill Jr.

His sidekick for the Japanese outreach was Bill Jr.'s West Coast man, the veteran Ken Clapp who easily assumed an ambassadorial role. "My on-the-ground leader," Brooks said. "Ken was very skilled in knowing the international community and also knowing the racing business."

Clapp remembers making 17 trips to Japan overall. He remembers one in particular, as do many others.

Gary Smith, NASCAR's current managing director of event logistics, was for years the head of NASCAR's marina near downtown Daytona Beach, Florida, where he supervised the maintenance of, among other vessels, Bill Jr.'s water craft. He was also Bill Jr.'s "skipper" for many a trip, and they grew very close through the years. Time on the water will facilitate that sort of thing. Smith said that as time passed, he felt more like a family member than an employee.

Gary Smith was on the flight to Narita with Bill Jr.

"A little bit before the trip, I remember Bill had been having a little bit of pain in his fingers," Smith said. "But he wanted to make the trip to Japan that year. Everybody else was already over there; he asked me if I wanted to go, I said sure since I'd never been to Japan, and we took off. Flew to Chicago first, then hopped on a JAL flight to Narita."

It was a fun trip—for awhile. A couple of drinks—and a couple of watches. "They came around on the plane selling watches," Smith said. "Bill bought us one apiece.

"When we arrived and got off the plane, I noticed he was walking slowly, but I didn't think much about it at first because he would sometimes walk slowly anyway. But by the time we reached customs, he was pasty white. He looked at me and said in that distinctive voice of his, 'Pal, I don't feel so good.' I got him to sit down because he was getting worse and worse."

Bill Jr. had suffered a heart attack due to an arterial blockage. Rushed by ambulance to a former military hospital, he was fortunate to be treated by an especially talented physician, a graduate from one of Japan's best medical schools.

"He was really top-notch," Smith said.

A stent was inserted to rectify the blockage.

"Then we were stuck for awhile," Smith said. "The hospital had protocol which was going to require we stay there for something like a month. This was an old hospital. No TV. No phone lines. As you can imagine, when Bill started feeling better, he wanted to get out of there. He was going nuts.

"In addition to the protocol issue, there also was the cultural issue where the doctor can't 'lose face' by us leaving."

Whereupon they began to mastermind Bill Jr.'s "escape" and transfer to another hospital. And how perfect was this: a longtime corporate partner of

NASCAR's got involved—Coca-Cola offered whatever resources necessary to help with the situation. Given the circumstances, this was most refreshing.

"Coke has a huge presence in Japan," Smith continued, "and they helped get Bill out of there under the pretense that he was an important American businessman and that the hospital in Narita didn't have adequate enough facilities to enable him to conduct business during his stay. Which was true. So we were able to move him to St. Luke's Hospital in Tokyo. That allowed the doctor to save face since Bill was leaving not because of him but because of the hospital."

Paul Brooks said he'll "never forget the knock on my hotel door in Suzuka and then being told Bill had had a heart attack and was in a hospital in Narita. When you hear those kinds of words…and then compound that with the realities of international travel…the language barrier, unknown hospitals. It's one thing if you have an emergency when you're in Daytona or Charlotte where you know the community real well, but when you're somewhere like Japan and you find out your leader is down, well, it's a pretty big shock."

True to one of Bill Jr.'s credos borrowed from the entertainment business, the show indeed went on, and while NASCAR's boss was recovering, a significant event transpired. During the NASCAR Thunder Special-Suzuka, there were several firsts logged. Cars practiced and qualified in the rain using Goodyear's new rain tire developed especially for the 3,400-pound Winston Cup machines, and cars were equipped with windshield wipers and rear running lights. A European-style qualifying format featured six groups of drivers, five per group, each group getting three laps, with the fast laps setting the positions. Mark Martin earned the pole and led 51 of the 125 laps, but it was the previous season's Rookie of the Year, Mike Skinner, who won the race in his Richard Childress–owned Chevrolet.

RCR driver Dale Earnhardt had nearly won the first Japan race the year before, losing by merely 1.192 seconds to Rusty Wallace; Skinner went on to win the final Cup exhibition in 1998, at the then-new Motegi Twin Ring complex. The Motegi event's lasting historical importance: Dale Earnhardt and his son, Dale Jr., competed together for the first time with the kid finishing sixth, two spots ahead of the seven-time champion.

Back home in Daytona Beach, while Bill Jr. was fidgeting in his hospital bed and Mike Skinner was taking the checkered flag, Betty Jane France was trying to determine if she needed to fly to Japan.

"I was going to go back to Daytona, get her, and bring her back to Tokyo," Clapp said. "But then Brian France and I got our heads together and figured that Bill wouldn't want us to make such a big fuss. So we chartered a plane, put a bunch of hospital stuff on it, a doctor, plus Lesa's husband, Dr. Bruce Kennedy, and took him back to Daytona."

Meanwhile, Paul Brooks, who had previously bought a state-of-the-art laptop in a major electronics shop, figured out how to transfer a digital camera image to the laptop—this was 1997, remember—and e-mailed the image to Betty Jane.

"It was a good way to connect them," Brooks said.

Three weeks later, Bill Jr. and Ken Clapp were having dinner at a five-star restaurant in Manhattan.

"Pretty amazing," Clapp said, about that night of apparent calm before what would turn out to be a decade of intermittent storms in the health of Bill France Jr.

Chapter Eighteen

The Chairman

On November 28, 2000, for the first time in the history of NASCAR, someone not named France held the title as the sanctioning body's president. It was a major development, but from the start of his new job, Mike Helton tempered discussion by reminding people, "You don't replace Bill Jr."

Helton's appointment accompanied the creation of the new NASCAR board of directors, headed of course by Bill France Jr. as the board's chairman and chief executive officer. The other board members were Bill Jr.'s son and brother, Brian and Jim; his daughter, Lesa Kennedy; and Helton.

In February 1999, Helton became the first person outside the France family to take over the day-to-day operations of NASCAR when he was named senior vice president and chief operating officer. Prior to his appointment, Helton was NASCAR's vice president for competition, a position he had held since 1994.

Creation of the NASCAR board was perhaps slightly overdue and partly resulted from Bill Jr. confronting his worsening health, which he openly acknowledged. After his heart attack in November 1997, he was diagnosed with cancer. Concurrently, he had become seriously hampered by dermatomyositis, a connective-tissue disease causing inflammation of the muscles and the skin. In his last year, the dermatomyositis at times would be more problematic than any of his other ailments.

"I didn't want to be 92 years old and still worrying about which flag was being thrown," Bill Jr. said on the day of the announcement. "Things are going to change. The health problems I've had woke some people up. Maybe we need to be better prepared. It was time to bring new blood on in a formal way. There is too much involved not to. What this does now is just formalize what we've been doing the past few years.

"We set the wheels in motion for this announcement when Mike was made senior VP. This is something that has to be done for the good of the sport. This is a progression from the so-called one-man czar to a more corporate structure. We have a full board of directors with all the authority the by-laws will permit. It's not an advisory board at all.

"This needed to happen."

Jim France reflected on the announcement and described it clearly as a watershed moment in NASCAR history.

"When Bill got sick, it was part of our planning to have a succession of leadership and training that we inherited from Mom and Dad," Jim said. "We had already started down that road…when Bill got sick, we stepped it up a little bit.

"We created several things to create a stable platform of management for NASCAR. Going forward, we didn't want things to rest on one individual's shoulders. We had expanded, grown quite a bit. At the same time, we had some talented people who had been with the company for quite awhile. As our business grew, it was more than a one-man show, [so] to speak. The plan was to make NASCAR like any other public company so that if the leader goes down, the continuity goes on. So we not only established a board of directors, but we also transferred the authority to the board."

A native of Bristol, Tennessee, Helton worked in radio before becoming public relations director at Atlanta Motor Speedway in 1980. Five years later, he became that track's general manager and in 1986 moved to NASCAR's affiliate company, International Speedway Corporation, to serve as general manager of Daytona International Speedway. Helton then became president of Talladega Superspeedway before sliding over to NASCAR in 1994 as vice president of competition.

On paper, Helton looked like a smart pick.

In person, even more so.

Helton's imposing physical stature, accented by a perpetual scowl, broom-thick mustache, and baritone voice, made him just the right sort of bad-ass dude to start patrolling the NASCAR garage area when Bill France Jr. was no longer able to do so. Soon, Helton became renowned, just as Bill Jr. had, for his "meetings" with drivers and crew chiefs inside the NASCAR hauler—called, during the Winston sponsor days, the "big red hauler."

"Big Mike"—President George W. Bush, among others, called him that—would soon become an ass-kicker in his own right, doing Bill Jr. and the memory of Big Bill France proud.

"Becoming president was just kinda dumb luck for me," Helton said. "Back when I was running the track at Atlanta, I got to know NASCAR's decision-makers. At that time, NASCAR had probably less than a handful of people who got everything done.

"It was 1985 and I was in an environment where I needed to make a change [in employment]. Back then, for most track operators, racing was a sideline or a hobby. The one group that made a living out of the business and depended on the business to make it was the France family."

After expressing a desire to leave Atlanta to NASCAR vice presidents Jim Hunter and Les Richter, Helton got a job offer from ISC. And then eight years later, he got another: Bill France Jr. wanted him to run Talladega, a facility that held a special place in the sport's history—and Bill Jr.'s heart.

"That ramped up my experience with Bill Jr., running a track where Bill was really hands-on," Helton said.

Helton learned all about being hands-on when he came to NASCAR in '94, replacing Richter, the former NFL great who became one of NASCAR's most effective—and popular—executives to run the competition department.

"As vice president of competition, I did all memberships, all sanctioning agreements, handled competition issues, scheduling issues, a lot of the fundamental operational things NASCAR does to put race cars on the race tracks. That wasn't indicative of what *I* did; it was indicative of what the sport did. I inherited those responsibilities from Les Richter. He had to do all the same things I had to.

"But as the sport got bigger, and the responsibilities increased, Bill Jr. recognized there needed to be a better organized NASCAR to handle all that. He saw the growth coming and understood NASCAR needed to do it right, and in order to do it right, it took a broader organization.

"So I go from being vice president of competition...to senior vice president...to chief operating officer...to president—in an era that was not about Mike Helton but rather about the sport getting bigger, about Brian France coming along, making a lot of impact on things that made NASCAR able to grow. During that period of time, responsibility for running NASCAR was evolving from resting on one set of shoulders, which Bill Jr. represented, to a broader set of shoulders."

Pragmatism again ruled the day, even if the day was growing slightly darker for Bill Jr.

Face to face with his own mortality, Bill Jr. stared it down.

"He accepted reality more than anyone, and I always admired him for that," Helton said. "Whether he liked it or agreed with it, life was what it was. He knew the transfer of responsibility, the transfer of leadership, of knowledge, of experience, and of ideas was critical because, as he often said, 'Man's the only animal that walks the face of the Earth who knows he's gonna die.' He was very committed to the responsibility for what his father created and what he had built and grown for the next generation. He wanted to be sure that 10 generations from now, everything was still right with NASCAR."

This reality led to the selection of Mike Helton as NASCAR's third president. And on the day the selection was announced, Bill Jr. sounded not in the least like an old man yearning for the past. In the autumn of 2000, he was still mashing the gas.

"It's time, I think, to bring some new blood on board in a formal way," France said. "This sport needs to press on. And we're *going* to press on."

Section V

The Last Laps
(2001–07)

Chapter Nineteen

Fighting Back

Bill France Jr. stepped down, so to speak, from NASCAR's presidency and then stepped back to catch his breath. Better at that point to leave the new president, Mike Helton, to fight many of the battles Bill Jr. had once relished.

Bill Jr. had new battles on the horizon.

The heart attack in Japan ended up being the first item in a long list of medical challenges. Well, check that: Actually, Bill Jr. had a horrendous boating accident in Daytona Beach back in April 1990, severely breaking both ankles when his Boston Whaler fishing boat jumped a swell while jetting through an inlet en route to the Atlantic Ocean. The boat planted hard into the water. Bill Jr. was standing, and his ankles took the brunt of the landing.

After the Japan trip, however, he was faced with:

The diagnosis of dermatomyositis and prostate cancer in August 1999, and a lung cancer diagnosis in December 1999.

Diabetes, a troubling ailment that he considered more of an annoyance than an illness, surfaced. He responded with a less-than-serious maintenance of the disease, which did not help matters.

And in August 2002, a heart bypass operation that came about after a nasty fall outside a Jacksonville, Florida, restaurant, in which Bill Jr. suffered a broken hip. He had been having dinner with the late Bob Snodgrass, a great friend from the sports car racing scene. (Snodgrass died in April 2007, only two months before Bill Jr.'s death.)

During examinations prior to surgery to repair the hip, the need for the bypass was discovered. "Just one thing after another," lamented Betty Jane France.

It has been said that Bill Jr. came by his ailments honestly. His penchant for hot dogs and other fast foods was complemented by a several-pack-a-day cigarette habit for years, a habit that no doubt got some help from the 33 years of Winston sponsorship. Throw in the very occasional scotch and a non-existent exercise regimen, and the late-life illnesses were not surprising.

Neither was it surprising to anyone close to Bill France Jr. how hard he fought during the last decade of his life to keep living. On the other hand, doctors were more than surprised—they were stunned. At the time of the lung cancer diagnosis in 1999, he was given six months to a year to live.

"He defied that," said his longtime secretary Geri McMullin.

Added Rick Hendrick: "Absolutely the toughest man I've ever seen. Despite all the problems he had walking, breathing. He never gave up hope. He refused to quit. He'd always tell me, 'The genie's still in the bottle.'

"And he also refused to stop talking about things that were important to him—and that was the sport."

Hendrick made a number of trips to Daytona Beach to visit Bill Jr., returning a favor from years earlier. When Hendrick was fighting leukemia, Bill Jr. stayed in touch steadily, be it by phone or in person, offering support.

Gary Smith was around Bill Jr. a lot in those later years. For a while he stayed with Bill Jr. and Betty Jane to assist with care. The dermatomyositis made his muscles so weak that he sometimes could not get out of bed without help, much less make it to and from the car to travel to the Mayo Clinic in Jacksonville for treatments.

"A lot of people likened his personality to John Wayne [Bill Jr.'s idol]—a real, All-American tough guy," Smith said. "He liked having that tough-guy persona, too. He didn't like to show the tender side of himself, which he did have."

Bill Jr., while fighting for his life, still managed to make friends wherever he went. One was his oncologist, Dr. William Maples of the Mayo Clinic, who told Betty Jane France that he learned more from Bill Jr. than he learned at medical school. Maples wrote the following letter to NASCAR (it has been edited for length) for this book:

"It was my privilege and honor to participate in Mr. France's medical care and life journey from December 1999 through June 2007. Physicians continuously learn from their patients not only about medical conditions, but also about life in general. Reflecting on my many visits with Mr. France, themes of generosity, honesty, courage and will, humor, and love are vividly present....

"There was a theme of generosity: Mr. France took every opportunity to share the blessings bestowed on him and his family with me, my family and friends, the city of Daytona Beach, the State of Florida, and the country....

"There was a theme of honesty: Through all of my interactions with Mr. France, both in and away from medical care, I greatly appreciated the honesty and integrity of our relationship. There was never any doubt about Mr. France's 'true north,' and his actions matched his words.

"Courage and will: A conversation I had with Mr. France during a hospitalization remains etched in my mind. Mr. France was quite ill at the time and had fought hard for weeks without a clear light at the end of the tunnel. He appropriately was considering stopping further medical intervention, and when I explained that there continued to be some glimmer of hope and asked that he continue the fight, his courage, will, and determination peaked. Through the honesty and trust we built, he continued his fight, and we were all blessed with several more years of life and service to his family, friends, and country. What a demonstration of extraordinary courage!

"There was humor: Through the seriousness of his medical condition, not a visit passed where he did not share some humor about his life, family, or business. The humor broke down barriers that could exist with a man of his greatness....

"And, there was love: Although a first impression of Mr. France may be one of a serious, no-nonsense, and somewhat stern individual, it became readily apparent the heart that Mr. France had for his family, friends, community, and country. Mr. France realized the impact that he had on so many people and made his decisions from the mind and heart. Although his honesty and expectations may have created tough-love situations, his actions were laced with the love he had for people. It was refreshing for me to see the joy he experienced when extending this love to those around him.

"One of the gifts of being a physician is to take part in the lives of so many individuals who come from so many different walks of life but share the same vulnerability of human life. Participating in this journey with Mr. France over seven years provided me invaluable life lessons."

"Bill was going to fight it until the end," Betty Jane France said of the cancer struggles. "I think anybody who has cancer has that ability to fight, the hope that they're going to make it. I think that's what he had—he thought he was really going to beat it. And he had the hardest of treatments, chemo and radiation

111

both at one time. It was so hard on his body, but he was going to do it. I don't think I could've gone through what he went through."

Betty Jane acknowledged there was a purposeful secrecy surrounding Bill Jr.'s health problems, especially regarding the cancer diagnoses. The media speculated from the outset that he was stricken with lung cancer, and the guilt-by-association label was quickly stuck to Winston. For anyone with the slightest bit of anti-tobacco inclination, the cruel irony was impossible to ignore. (Bill Jr. quit smoking after his 1997 heart attack.)

"You knew what people were going to say when Bill got cancer: 'Well, he smokes!' But he just didn't want the finger pointed at anybody. He knew people would blame R.J. Reynolds.

"We didn't have any privacy, and there are some things that you just have to have privacy about. And, while I don't like smoking now, I used to be a smoker, and I feel like that's a person's right if they want to smoke. I think we just didn't want the press—which can be brutal sometimes—to know all about it.

"It was an awful time."

There were a number of awful times during Bill Jr.'s decline.

"It was sad to see," said NASCAR vice president Jim Hunter. "Here Bill was at a point in his life where he could've and should've been enjoying life. But he couldn't. It just goes to show you how important your health is."

There were rebounds, however, some that appeared nearly miraculous and they restored him to the point where he often simply looked like a man in his late 60s or early 70s, not someone who was that old and fighting off life-threatening diseases. And of course his mind always remained sharp—as did his tongue.

Felix Sabates can supply a living, breathing, laughing testament to that fact.

In July 2000, Bill Jr. was admitted to St. Luke's Hospital in Jacksonville after a check-up at Mayo. Things did not look good. He was close to death. Even he thought the end was near.

After a phone call from Mike Helton, Sabates and Rick Hendrick flew down to Jacksonville to see Bill Jr. and pay their last respects.

"We were coming to tell Bill good-bye," Sabates said.

The night before Sabates got there, Bill Jr. had given Gary Smith his new Swiss watch, a Corum worth thousands of dollars. He said he wanted Smith to have the watch after all the care—and caring—he had provided. Sabates had heard about this.

Sabates had also heard about Bill's recent purchase of a new Lexus.

"We got into his room and Bill looked terrible, his head was terribly swollen from the chemo and the radiation," Sabates said. "I was sitting on the bed, and I grabbed his hand. My ex-wife was with me, and she was sitting on the other side of the bed. We were talking to Bill, but his eyes were closed. He was like he was in a coma.

"I leaned down close to him and said, 'Hey Bill, shit, if you're going to give anything else away like you did the watch, can I have the Lexus?' Immediately, he squeezed my hand really hard and half-whispered, 'Fuck you.'

"Right then, I said, well, he ain't going nowhere yet. I told people that, and they didn't believe me.

"We were somewhere together about a month after that and he asked me, 'You sonofabitch, did you really want to get my car?'

"I said, 'No Bill, I just wanted to see if you were paying attention.'"

Chapter Twenty

Television

Coming into the 2001 season, things were about to change regarding NASCAR's presence on television sets across America and throughout the world. Change was on the way because the power of television, and everything it could do for NASCAR, was not lost on Bill France Jr.

Ever.

Long-time newspaper reporter and columnist Al Pearce tells a story a bit later in this book (Chapter 24: Media) about Bill Jr.'s reaction to the famous 1979 fight between Cale Yarborough and the Allison brothers at the end of the 1979 Daytona 500, the first time the 500 had been broadcast flag-to-flag. Bill Jr. was simply overjoyed at the exposure the fight received.

After all, no one had gotten hurt; it was more of a scuffle than a battle.

And the amount of publicity was massive.

Television coverage of NASCAR picked up in the ensuing years but continued to be a lap down, as it were, compared to America's more traditional sports. For years, fans of the National Football League knew that each Sunday, NFC games would be on CBS and AFC games on NBC—holdovers from the days before the NFL-AFL merger. Today, while the conference contract deals have shifted around and there are more night-game telecasts, football fans still know that all the games are going to be delivered by the *major* networks and at typically uniform times. (NASCAR actually got away from consistent starting times in the 2000s before fan input helped lead to a return to more standard times beginning with the 2010 season.)

Bill Jr. coveted NFL-caliber stature on television for NASCAR. And in the late 1990s, with his health failing for the first time in his life, he empowered his son Brian and his other bright young leaders to go out and make it happen. NASCAR senior vice president Paul Brooks was part of that team.

"As was typical in a number of the big initiatives and opportunities that were evolving in potential for the sport at that time, there was an interesting set of dynamics at work in NASCAR," Brooks said.

"You had Brian coming into the business in a significant way. Bill was on the top of his career—and the world. You had what I call a very healthy tension. Brian had just an amazing vision and understanding of all things sponsorship, licensing, and marketing, and at the same time you had the amazing wisdom of Bill France Jr., who had helped shape so many elements of the sport through the years. Bill, who was very, very hands-on in all aspects of TV, was really the lead guy in all areas for TV for years. He was the guy the networks knew. Bill Jr. was *the* guy. *The* man. There was a strong foundation there with and in the top broadcast networks. Bill had the aura, the respect."

On November 11, 1999, NASCAR announced the blockbuster "consolidated" deal that had its roots in the 1979 Daytona 500. The deal, commencing in 2001, was for six years with four entities paying an approximate total of $2.4 billion starting with the 2001 season: NBC, Turner (TNT), FOX, and FX. The vast majority of the races would be on NBC and FOX. Collectively, the contract tripled the number of NASCAR Sprint Cup (then Winston Cup) races to be shown.

It was a dramatic departure from the past; previously, individual tracks had negotiated individual TV deals. It took some selling by Bill Jr., Brian, and everyone involved to convince tracks to buy in to the new approach that ultimately would provide much greater financial rewards than the previous fragmented way of doing TV business.

NBS Sports Chairman Dick Ebersol said on that day, "NASCAR's ratings went up, and they did it despite having numerous partners. It was hard for the sport to have a regular platform. It was hard for fans to find the races. With our new platforms, this is going to be an awesome change for NASCAR fans."

"This is a historic day, and it captures our vision of NASCAR's future," Bill Jr. said. "This will showcase NASCAR racing to millions of sports fans like never before, bringing them closer to NASCAR in ways they could have never imagined.

"By doing this, we're going to take our sport throughout America into people's homes."

USA Today described the deal as part of "NASCAR continuing to morph itself into a sporting entity that has forsaken a moonshine identity for a mainstream plunge."

Compliment or criticism? Hard to say. But there was recognizable criticism from some traditionalists about former partners CBS, ESPN, ABC, and TNN being replaced. And to be fair, the criticism was somewhat understandable. CBS, after all, had become home to the Daytona 500 and other major events since the epic 1979 event in part because of the recognizable voice of commentator Ken Squier. ABC's relationship with NASCAR dated to the 1960s and the televising of portions of races on the famed Wide World of Sports show. ESPN and TNN (The Nashville Network) were relatively new to the fold, but each played a valuable role in reaching the core fan base as complements to the major networks' broadcasts.

Bill Jr. acknowledged the criticism but was also quick to point out that NASCAR was, after all, a business. Bids were offered. The best bids won out. He didn't talk financial specifics, but he made it clear that there were major differences in some of the offers. "Free market ruled the day," he said. He indicated that if critics were privy to the specifics of the bidding process, they would drop their opposition in a heartbeat.

And so the new era of NASCAR on television began with the first race of the season in 2001, the Daytona 500—22 years after ol' Cale and Bobby and Donnie wrestled around in the grass between Turns 3 and 4, not even noticing that their old rival Richard Petty, that opportunistic SOB, was rocketing by en route to his seventh victory in NASCAR's greatest race.

February 18, 2001, was set up to be one of the greatest days in NASCAR history. No doubt about that. NASCAR was going big time, and everybody was along for the ride. All one needed to do to figure that out was check out the entry blanks during the 2001 season and compare the total purse money to previous years. A good portion of the rights fees rolling in were mostly going to roll right back out to the industry. The announced division of the TV revenue was 65 percent to track owners, 25 percent to drivers, and 10 percent to NASCAR.

And then came the final, fateful lap of that Daytona 500. One of NASCAR's greatest days immediately became one of its darkest. Dale Earnhardt's Turn 4 crash and immediate death shook NASCAR to its core. On a personal level, outside of Earnhardt's immediate family, chances are few people were more shaken than Bill France Jr. The driver he called "Sunday Money," who had won seven championships and made things like an eight-year television deal possible, was gone.

Whereupon NASCAR took off.

The next race at North Carolina Motor Speedway had a rating of 8.2—8.2 for Rockingham! NASCAR had gone from sport to spectacle in one week. Clearly the spike was due to the sudden increased national interest because of Earnhardt's death. Ratings would settle back to normal levels, but the growth of the sport would continue and television would be the catalyst.

"Bill saw all that was coming," Brooks said. "The TV deal was about benefiting the entire industry, not just NASCAR. This was about an initiative that could have profound effects on the sport."

Chapter Twenty-One

Earnhardt

Going into the 2001 Daytona 500, there seemed to be potential for the race to rank right up there with the 1979 Daytona 500, the 1984 Firecracker 400, and the inaugural race at Indianapolis in 1994. The 2001 Daytona 500 was going to be *big*, the kick-off event for the landmark network television contract.

The 500 that day drew a network Nielsen rating of 10; more than 10 million households tuned in, equating to nearly 18 million viewers or, as Bill Jr. liked to say, nearly 18 million "sets of eyeballs." All those figures would be substantial increases compared to 2000, the swan song for the Daytona 500's long-time standard-bearer, CBS. Collectively, those foreshadowed NASCAR's imminent popularity growth.

With the stage set, with all those people watching at home—not to mention the 200,000 or so jammed into the Daytona International Speedway—NASCAR's theatre turned tragic. When seven-time NASCAR Sprint Cup champion Dale Earnhardt right-turned into the Turn 4 wall on the race's last lap and died instantaneously, the sport of NASCAR was shaken to its core—as was a 67-year-old man fighting for his own life. Bill France Jr. watched one of NASCAR's darkest days unfold from the control tower, perched high above the expansive 2.5-mile tri-oval he and his father had built 42 years before.

And then he braced for the storm that was surely coming, a storm that would preface even further growth of NASCAR despite the loss of the man Bill Jr. called that night "our greatest driver."

∽

When the sun rose on the morning of February 19, 2001, NASCAR had been changed forever. Earnhardt's death immediately sparked debate over the use of head and neck restraints in NASCAR, devices which at the time were

118

recommended but not mandated. Earnhardt himself had been steadfastly opposed to the devices and was seen as a maverick of sorts when it came to safety. He had a seat set-up that was lower than most drivers. He disdained the use of a full-face helmet, preferring an old-school open-face model. And in general, he had been quoted a number of times where he equated concern with safety as synonymous with a lack of courage on a driver's part.

His death, however, called everything into question—starting with NASCAR itself.

In the week leading up to the 2001 Daytona 500, the *Chicago Tribune* had published a series on auto racing safety and, in some cases, the perceived lack thereof. No form of motorsports was immune, and all were criticized in some manner by the lead writer of the series, Ed Hinton. NASCAR took perhaps the most lumps, with the recent deaths of three drivers highlighted—Adam Petty, Kenny Irwin, and Tony Roper—and suggestions that all three lives could've been saved if the drivers had been wearing head and neck restraints.

With Earnhardt's death coming on the same day that the *Tribune's* series concluded, the resulting media feeding frenzy was inevitable. An additional controversy then emerged that exacerbated the situation. In the days after the accident, NASCAR announced that a safety belt had separated in Earnhardt's car during the accident, although emergency worker Tommy Propst, who worked the scene, said he did not remember such a separation.

There was more. The *Orlando Sentinel,* part of the *Tribune* chain, was one of a number of media outlets who sued for access to the Earnhardt autopsy photos. That collective request was ultimately denied.

NASCAR was clearly under siege and announced the beginning of a full-scale investigation into Earnhardt's death with a late-summer target for conclusion.

When the NASCAR Sprint Cup Series returned to Daytona in July for the annual summer event, Bill Jr. and NASCAR president Mike Helton agreed to an interview on MSNBC with anchor Brian Williams. It could've gone better in terms of public perception, as Bill Jr.'s plaintive, always pragmatic manner was misconstrued by some as brusque.

At one point, when asked about NASCAR's credibility being called into question regarding the seat belt issue, Bill Jr. contentiously responded to Williams—a longtime friend to NASCAR who was asking some tough questions, as he of course had to do.

"The first thing is, we have not lied," Bill Jr. said. "And the second thing is, there have been some corrections. We may have made some comments that we have regretted, but it's never been our intention to lie…it's all going to be on the table in August."

The Earnhardt Investigation, as it came to be called, had the approval of Bill Jr. contrary to the notion that it was force-fed past an ailing leader. John Cassidy, a legal counsel to NASCAR, ISC, and the Frances since the early 1960s, recalled clearly the desire by Bill Jr. to examine Earnhardt's death via a full-blown look into what exactly happened out in Turn 4.

"NASCAR had had wrecks and deaths before, but this was sort of like Joe DiMaggio getting hit by a ball standing at the plate and being killed," Cassidy said. "It was very difficult to believe that Dale Earnhardt had died.

"When you looked at replays of the accident on TV, it did not look as threatening as it turned out to be. So, what you had first of all was the shock that your biggest star had been killed, and then you had everybody wondering *how* it could happen.

"Bill Jr. was concerned not only for the Earnhardt family but the millions of fans who had watched their hero get killed. It was very, very tough. We were all in a state of shock…it's hard to describe the atmosphere at the time.

"So what do you do? We had a number of discussions, and it became obvious that in his death he was greater as a public figure than a lot of people realized. I think a number of people were taken aback by the outpouring of grief. So we were faced with the question, 'What were we going to do about this?'

"Bill Jr. picked up on that thread. He felt there should be a review. He thought we had to bring some closure to this awful development. He also thought we needed to know in greater detail especially because the death was so befuddling. And also so we could see how to improve safety conditions in the future."

Added Brian France, "My dad wanted to find the right answers to the questions regarding what happened. He had some concerns how to go about that. He didn't want a witch hunt involving various experts and opinions. He wanted to make sure we weren't answering every criticism coming at us because we thought we had to. Rather, he wanted us to look hard at what had happened.

"The media had done a variety of exposés on us regarding the safety elements. His idea was they weren't aware of what we were doing already as far as safety was concerned. He didn't think we were getting a fair shake—and he might have been right.

"It was a difficult time."

George Pyne, now the president of the International Management Group, was NASCAR's senior vice president in 2001, three years into a seven-year stint with the organization, a period in which he spearheaded a number of modifications to the NASCAR business model that were considered revolutionary. Pyne worked in conjunction mainly with Brian France, who had by then risen to the role of executive vice president. Pyne was the ultimate NASCAR outsider. Born in Milford, Massachusetts, he attended an Ivy League school—Brown University, where he excelled on the football field as an offensive lineman. He was not the football player his father was; the "real George Pyne," as his son called him, played for the Boston Patriots in the old American Football League.

Pyne was a marketing madman—and a micro-manager of sorts. Meaning he had his eyes—if not his fingerprints—on all things NASCAR at all times.

Pyne was also brilliant as the driving force behind implementing the Earnhardt Investigation, an exhaustive six-month, multi-million-dollar project that culminated in a massive press conference at the Atlanta Hilton on August 21 of that year. The event laid out the details of just how Dale Earnhardt had died during a complex and compelling two-hour session headed by experts in the field of safety—Drs. James Raddin and Dean Sicking, the latter now renowned for development of the SAFER barrier ("soft wall") system in use at all NASCAR national series events.

Never had NASCAR bared its soul like this. Bill France Jr. had a tough time coming to grips with that aspect of the "new" NASCAR, a reaction that should've surprised no one. Bill Jr. may have approved the investigation, but he still considered it extraordinarily intrusive, while at the same time he understood that his sport's success had brought a media-driven microscope along for the ride.

"I'd say a couple of things about that period to provide some perspective," Pyne said. "Go back to 1994, Speedweeks at Daytona. Two drivers died—Rodney Orr and Neil Bonnett. Well, back then they cleaned up the track and kept on practicing and there were relatively few questions, relatively little media coverage about it.

"Safety, up until that point, was a cooperative effort between drivers and NASCAR. There were many, many different safety enhancements that came along through the years, some unfortunately coming along after a bad accident. The point being, there wasn't really a formalized safety process back then.

"Now, fast forward to 2001. The popularity of the sport was night-and-day compared to 1994. Scrutiny was unlike anything NASCAR had had before. So...

"When you lost your seven-time champion...

"In the Daytona 500...

"On the last lap...

"On national TV...

"With who-knows-how-many millions of people watching...

"Compared to 1994, it was a whole new ballgame—in two respects. No. 1, historically, NASCAR didn't really have the resources to invest in a formalized safety process. There was an informal process. It wasn't that people were callous to safety, but there were limited resources to be spent on the part of NASCAR, the teams—everybody. Therefore, it was more a reactive approach to safety rather than a proactive.

"No. 2, in terms of the communications side of the thing, in 2001 NASCAR was far more significant, with the Earnhardt story leading the morning news, the evening news.... *USA Today* and *Time* magazine broke sales records after his death. The race the week after the Daytona 500—at Rockingham, North Carolina—got an '8' TV rating. The focus was enormous. As Brian was telling us all back then, 'NASCAR is now on center stage.'

"So just seven years earlier, you had two drivers die and NASCAR had to say very little about it to anyone. Now, it was seven years later, and the world wanted a lot of details. The scrutiny level was a result of the success of NASCAR. We grew up all at once on center stage. That transition was tough for Bill and for all of us.

"But to Bill's credit, Brian's credit, and NASCAR's credit, millions of dollars were invested in the Research and Development Center, a state-of-the-art facility. No other sport has anything like that place. And today, NASCAR's safety record is impeccable.

"Whatever shortcomings that existed—which by the way were not because of callous neglect but rather just because that's the way things were done for years—NASCAR went from that to being very proactive in safety. It shows in the results. Now NASCAR has a pretty good record in an area where, in auto racing, you're not going to be perfect.

"While it was a trying time, a lot of good things came out of a very bad situation."

NASCAR commissioned a highly respected communications consulting firm in Washington, D.C., Powell Tate, to provide advice and guidance during the course of the investigation. One of the major ways that Powell Tate—headed by the late, former White House Press Secretary Jody Powell—would help was in the preparation for the nonstop media inquiries preceding the investigation and the questions that would be posed at the Atlanta press conference.

Leading up to the Atlanta event, NASCAR had a number of meetings at Powell Tate's offices. Bill Jr. attended periodically, and it is fair to say he accepted the somewhat arduous investigation process grudgingly. A story has emerged from one of the earliest meetings that aptly describes the atmosphere in a downtown D.C. office tower where a bunch of Washington insiders were trying to tell NASCAR how to run a portion of its public relations business.

A full-blown discussion was ongoing, led by Powell, about how to handle the tremendous spotlight that had shone on the sport since the tragic afternoon of February 18, 2001. The discussion turned somewhat contentious, and Bill Jr.'s frustration became obvious. Basically, he got mad as hell. Powell was ready with a reaction that immediately became a mantra for the balance of the investigative process—and a mantra that is still occasionally cited among longtime NASCAR employees who are privy to its origin.

"Bill," Powell began, "There are a lot of ways to deal with this situation. But being pissed off is not a plan."

The room went silent. No one talked to Bill France Jr. like that, least of all some guy who was part of a *Democratic* administration, for crying out loud.

Then, Bill France Jr. chuckled slightly. It was enough. Jody Powell, by God, had gotten through. From that moment forward, the rest of the process would not be easy but it would at least proceed.

And Powell would continue to get through, once telling Bill Jr. that "Kings of kingdoms and presidents of countries need to media train; you do, too."

Which Bill Jr. did, albeit grudgingly.

Just as the Talladega brouhaha had perhaps nudged Bill France Sr. toward taking a step back from the business, the death of Dale Earnhardt very easily could've had a similar effect on Bill Jr., although he never said so.

"Bill was devastated when Earnhardt died," Pyne said. "He was devastated also when we lost Adam Petty, Kenny Irwin, and Tony Roper not long before that. But with Earnhardt, they were obviously good friends."

Richard Childress, Earnhardt's longtime car owner, supplied a poignant viewpoint from those sad times saying, "It was very hard on Bill Jr. I met with him on that Sunday night when Dale died and spent that Monday together along with Mike Helton and a couple others.... Yeah, it was really tough for him, because he and Dale had a special relationship. They liked their boats and we'd all go fishing together. Whenever we did that, Bill was 'Captain Jack' to us. In fact, if Bill came on the radio during a race to talk to Dale, he'd always identify himself as that. He'd come on and say, 'This is Captain Jack here.'

"Me and Dale both had a special relationship with Bill Jr. He was as hard on us as anyone else when it came to the competition, but when the race was over he respected me and Dale's opinions. He could come and talk to us about things because he knew that we wanted what was best for the sport. He knew that the two of us wouldn't just be yanking his chain or, as he put it, 'pissing up his leg.'"

"Earnhardt's death had to take the starch out of Bill Jr.," said NASCAR vice president Jim Hunter. "He had come to really admire Earnhardt as a person, as a competitor, and as a businessman. He had a tremendous amount of respect for Earnhardt. They had a tremendous amount of respect for each other.

"I think Bill was proud to have Earnhardt involved in NASCAR because of Earnhardt's commitment, his dedication, his passion for the sport."

Yes, Hunter agreed, the death of the great champion could've very well had something to do with Bill Jr. stepping down. But Hunter points out that perhaps most important in the decision was the simple fact that the business of NASCAR was changing drastically—and daily.

Others close to Bill Jr. discount Earnhardt's death as a determining factor. Said one: "Bill was such a tough old SOB. I don't see that as being a reason. Earnhardt's death—Bill could handle that."

Perhaps. And if that last assessment is more accurate, then maybe it's just safe to say that Bill France Jr., ever the pragmatist, likely assessed all the changes and saw that it simply was time for the sport's leadership to change, as well.

It was time. Nothing more, nothing less.

Chapter Twenty-Two

Third Generation Takes Over

Brian France replacing his father as NASCAR's Chairman and CEO, while perhaps not an absolute lock, was about as predetermined as you get. Betty Jane France saw all along that her husband was forging a master plan to ensure that both their children would have a shot at leadership opportunities—and ultimately even more success than he achieved.

Their daughter, Lesa, was guided into the International Speedway Corporation fast lane all along. Likewise, Brian France motored along a NASCAR path, be it as a West Coast assistant of sorts to the venerable Ken Clapp, a track operator in Tucson, Arizona, or a budding licensing and marketing expert in Daytona Beach, Brian France was being groomed.

On the afternoon of September 13, 2003, Brian France's promotion to chairman and CEO at the age of 41 was announced (he would actually begin in that role the following month).

Bill Jr. was asked if there had ever been any doubt about his son replacing him.

"Why, absolutely not, or otherwise we wouldn't be doing it," Bill Jr. said.

And suddenly it was 1972 all over again. NASCAR's immediate doom was predicted by the harshest critics. In 2003, as in '72, the fact that the incoming boss had paid considerable dues for an extended period of time got short shrift.

"It goes with the territory," Brian said several years later. "You know you're going to get some criticism, partly because it's a family business and also because we're talking about a sport where people have a lot of opinions. Not every business would get so much scrutiny as this one got."

Coming into the job following not one but two legends, Brian France could've been excused for feeling the pressure and playing things close to the vest for however long he saw fit. Instead, he came out firing. The first indication that things were operating a bit differently: five days after the announcement of Brian's appointment, the long-running procedure of racing back to the yellow flag during cautions was abolished. Then, just after several months in charge, came a true bombshell. NASCAR announced in January 2004 that the long-running format for determining the NASCAR Sprint Cup Series champion was being replaced by a new, glitzier approach called the Chase for the NASCAR Sprint Cup.

The new format created a NASCAR "playoff system" of sorts. After 26 races, the top 10 (now it's the top 12) drivers in the series points advanced to the Chase. Their point totals were reset, with small increments separating them. They would then compete against each other, points-wise, for the championship over the last 10 races of the season.

The announcement followed a 2003 season that was largely devoid of drama, as the super-consistent Matt Kenseth built a substantial lead and basically coasted to the championship.

It was not the first time that sort of thing had happened.

Since 1972, there had been only a handful of seasons where the championship was decided at the season's final race, with many champions building up sizable leads with several weeks remaining in a given season. The Chase made such a snoozer scenario virtually impossible.

Which meant the Chase made sense, if NASCAR wanted to compete for sports fans' attention in the autumn against the World Series…the NFL, NBA, NHL, college football, and college basketball.

"When you're coming into a new situation like I was," Brian said, "you want to establish yourself and try to get some accomplishments that are your own. I know my Dad felt the same way back in 1972 when he took over, and he had a lot of accomplishments—over three decades, no less, which I probably won't try to do.

"Obviously you have to make smart decisions, but I think you have to get off to a good start and make progress."

Progress was one thing. The Chase, at first glance, was something else.

"My Dad thought it was real radical," Brian said. "I remember when I first told him about the idea, he told me to let him sleep on it, and we'd talk the next day. He acknowledged it was radical, let's say, in his *own* way. But I think he knew it was something I wanted to do. He was trying to be supportive of my leadership, and in the end he was always supportive—not only of me but of anybody who was trying to lead and trying to have responsibility and expectations attached to them. He knew you had to give people some room to fail or to succeed. He was pretty good about that…no, he was *really* good about that."

∞

When the announcement of Brian's takeover was made, Bill Jr.'s support was obvious. One got the feeling the old man was trying to pave the way for the young man, knowing that the same opposition he'd faced in 1972 would surface in updated form, heightened by the modern-day sensibilities of the various constituencies participating in the sport.

"Brian has worked long and hard for this opportunity, just as I had when I took over the reins from my father," Bill Jr. said. "He's earned his chance, and I know how important that is to him and to me. Brian has worked in about every area of the company, including running a race track, and he has exceeded my expectations each time. And I am a pretty tough critic."

Big surprise there, people were thinking.

"Brian is prepared and ready to lead our sport and company into the future," Bill Jr. continued. "The fact of the matter is, the NASCAR board would not have selected Brian for this role if we didn't think he was capable. There's too much at stake. In the past few years, we have seen a lot of changes for the betterment of our sport. We've seen a lot of innovation and new thinking. Many of these innovations happened because of Brian's prodding and passion for our sport.

"The role of a CEO and chairman is to be forward-looking, anticipating the challenges of tomorrow. Brian fits that role for NASCAR, and that's why I am recommending him to take on this new challenge.

"We had some challenges coming along when I took over from my father back in 1972. There were a few rough spots as we moved ahead. I kind of wanted to do things a new way, and he thought maybe the old way…my father thought the old way was as good as any. But we agreed on about everything.

"I think history shows that the sport's moved along pretty good. I think the same thing is going to happen on this go-around…. This had to happen sooner or later. I have total confidence in what Brian can do. He's loaded with street smarts, amongst other things. I'm very confident in what he can do. When I came in, I thought I was pretty relaxed in what I thought I could do. Then I let history speak for itself, from that standpoint."

127

Which is exactly what Brian Zachary France has done. During the last four years of his father's life, the new boss meshed pretty damn well with the old boss.

Bill France Jr. expected as much. He was proud of his son and all that he had achieved long before taking over NASCAR's top spot. And he was absolutely convinced there would be more achievements to come.

The kid he had fired so many times had come of age.

"We had our father-son moments," Brian said. "But in the end he was my greatest champion. And there's not a day goes by that I don't miss his guidance."

Chapter Twenty-Three

Speeches

Bill France Jr. enjoyed giving speeches and prepared accordingly, working in concert with various NASCAR staff members through the years but always making sure the words were ultimately his—either literally or conceptually.

Bill Jr., especially in his later years, liked to start the speech-writing process with a small meeting during which he would outline what he wanted to say. He was very meticulous about this, preparing for even the shortest of talks in a painstaking fashion with repeated drafts if needed. One of his trademarks was noticing, in an initial speech draft, even the slightest omission of the original talking points he had outlined. Another was noticing any—*any*—edits he had made on early drafts being ignored or "recast" on subsequent drafts. "You tried to sneak that one by me," he might say, peering over his reading glasses at his writer, saying no more because there was no need. The point had been made.

Bill Jr.'s speeches were sometimes spiced with witticisms that over the years became known as "Billisms." They were short and often politically incorrect, especially over the last two decades when workplace sensibilities experienced a seismic shift in what was considered appropriate language or behavior. But no matter how they were perceived in that vein, they likewise were universally understood whenever they were uttered. Billisms always had a basis in factually sound, reasonable assumptions or explanations. They were homespun philosophies spiced by colorful language and a larger-than-life personality. They were delivered, at once, with humor and authority. The effect could be overwhelming for those on the receiving end.

One of Bill Jr.'s favorites to describe the importance of everyone "being on the same page" when it came to an idea or initiative was, "We gotta all be pissing through the same straw."

There are more.

When Bill Jr. perceived someone as being all about style but lacking substance, they were called "all cowboy hat and no cattle."

When someone presented an idea he didn't like and he wanted to leave it behind during a discussion, he applied this analogy. "That idea is like a monkey's asshole. It'll start looking better only when it gets farther on up the tree."

When an employee would suggest a business model that seemed overdone and was missing the focus on NASCAR's main purpose—the racing itself—Bill loved bring people back down to Earth by using a saying that originated with former ISC board member Buz Baggett, who owned a funeral home in Daytona Beach. "In these situations," Bill Jr. would tell his ambitious employee, "Buz would say, 'I've been in the funeral business for 40 years, and I've never wanted to own the flower shop.'"

Buz Baggett's line had been transformed into a Billism. Bill Jr. put it to good use through the years.

He was fond of building a "library" of potential items that might be included in a future speech or letter. In his files, he kept a 33-page printout titled, "Insulting Sarcasm: Insulting quotes from famous persons who weren't afraid to speak their minds."

This document has Bill France Jr. written all over it. Check out these gems:

"He's so snobbish he has an unlisted zip code."
"He's very clever, but sometimes his brains go to his head."
"He is a self-made man and worships his creator."
And here is perhaps the best of the bunch, provided by Oscar Wilde: "The man has no enemies, but he is immensely disliked by his friends."

For his speeches, which typically were a mixture of the requisite corporate-driven messages and down-home straight talk, Bill Jr. drew upon sayings, quotations, even poems for his speeches. Yes, Bill France Jr., the tough-as-nails leader of the rough-house sport of stock car racing, enjoyed some poetry from time to time. He had a favorite poem by the great 19th century American poet Edward Rowland Sill called "Opportunity," a piece about medieval battle which he considered a metaphor for the success of the NASCAR business model. Leave it to Bill Jr. While the rest of the industry was voraciously reading things like *National Speed Sports News*—and make no mistake, he read that, too—he was getting into poetry.

"Opportunity" served as the central theme in a speech Bill Jr. gave in the spring of 2004 at his induction into the International Motorsports Hall of Fame. A portion of that speech follows, along with selected passages from other key speeches he gave through the years.

International Motorsports Hall of Fame Induction
Talladega, Alabama
May 2004

It's a great honor to be here tonight on a professional level and even more so on a personal level. Tonight, I get to see my name listed next to the man who laid the groundwork for everything I've been able to accomplish, Bill France Sr.

NASCAR is moving fast these days, on and off the track.

Our sport has grown tremendously to the point where sometimes it's hard to imagine the days, many years ago, when NASCAR was basically a two-man operation run by my father and his right-hand man at the time, Pat Purcell.

They did it all. And they did it well.

When I think of how they forged on in the face of adversity and uncertainty, I'm reminded of a poem by a fellow named Edward Sill. It's called 'Opportunity.'

The poem is about a great battle and how a brave soldier was wounded and lost his weapon. On the edge of the battlefield, a coward had given up the fight, snapped his sword in two, flung it to the ground, and run away. The coward's sword was crude and blunt, nothing like the precision blue-steel blade the brave soldier had lost. But when the brave soldier came upon that sword half-buried in the dirt, he snatched it up and carried on the fight.

Here's how the writer put it:

'With battle-shout, lifted afresh, he hewed his enemy down...and saved a great cause that heroic day.'

In simple terms, the soldier saw an opportunity and made the most of it.

That was the way my father approached things—decisively and bravely.

We need to remember those days, the battles fought, and the opportunities sought. And we should acknowledge how important those days were to building what we enjoy today.

Thank you.

Retirement of Reverend Hal Marchman
Daytona Beach, Florida
July 2004

The Reverend Hal Marchman has been a fixture on the NASCAR landscape for many years, as many of you know. He has been giving pre-race invocations at Daytona since we started racing here in 1959. In the process, his voice has become synonymous with the speedway.

In fact, it's not truly a Daytona race weekend until you hear Hal give what has become his signature sign-off: 'Shalom and Amen.'

Along the way, while becoming part of what we like to call the NASCAR Family, he also has become, simply, a good friend.

He was an especially good friend back when we decided we wanted to race on Sundays at Darlington Raceway. The state legislature actually had to change a state law to allow that to happen. Many members of the local religious communities, however, weren't too happy about Sunday stock car racing, and believe me, we heard from them. But then, they started hearing from Hal and his wife, Mary, who went up there and helped smooth things over. Hal spoke to his fellow pastors about all the good racing did for the area in terms of economic impact.

He emphasized how it was fine family entertainment.

He also reminded them that the Sunday races would start after church services were through.

And he talked a large number of church members into bringing their kids to the races. Once they got out there and had such a good time, they were more receptive to the notion of racing on Sunday.

He was there when we needed him. I guess you could say that's always been the case with Hal Marchman.

For years, whenever one of our drivers has had to go to the infield care center or over to Halifax Medical Center, Hal has been there. He has offered support, prayers—and friendship—to the driver, the driver's teammates, and of course, the driver's family. In the process, Hal has made some tough times a lot easier for a lot of people.

I have to admit, though, there was one time that we needed Hal Marchman and he wasn't there.

I don't recall the exact circumstances, but at one of our races here at Daytona in the early 1960s, Hal got to the track late and wasn't able to give the invocation.

'No problem,' my father Bill France Sr. said.

Bill Sr. figured that since he founded NASCAR, built the speedway, and even raced cars himself for awhile, he could surely handle an invocation.

And he did handle it well, actually. Until he got to the finish.

For whatever reason, Bill Sr. decided to put his own personal stamp on his public conversation with the Lord. Instead of Amen—much less 'Shalom and Amen'—he concluded the invocation this way:

'Sincerely yours, Bill France!'

After that, I can assure you of this: We never underestimated the importance of Hal Marchman.

I can also assure you of this: We made sure Hal never missed another invocation.

Chris Economaki Roast
July 1995

Chris used to host a dinner at his home the night after the Winston Cup banquet in New York. It was the only time in my life I've ever seen Chris pick up the tab for dinner.

Through the years, Chris' voice during races he worked on TV was unfortunately unforgettable. During live telecasts, he loved to put the spotlight on some of NASCAR's deficiencies. Now that Chris isn't on TV all the time anymore, is it any wonder that our sport has grown so much?

Celebration on the Hill 2006
Washington, D.C.
September 2006

(Note: Bill France Jr. was unable to attend this event hosted by the American Cancer Society Cancer Action Network. The event celebrated cancer survivorship and was aimed at empowering survivors and others to advocate for laws to help battle cancer. Bill Jr. addressed the function via a specially prepared video message.)

I consider myself a cancer survivor. I have periodic checkups, and when I come back from those, I tell my friends and family members that 'the genie is still in the bottle,' which is sort of our code for saying everything is okay. But it's also our way of putting a light-hearted touch on a serious subject.

Suffice to say I have a pretty good first-hand understanding of just how serious a subject cancer is and why the fight against the disease is so important.

Borrowing a phrase from my business, 'the checkered flag' is in sight in the fight against cancer. But that checkered flag is also a bit down the road. As we race to win this battle, we must not slow down. Indeed, now is the time to accelerate our efforts. If we all work together, the possibilities are endless and the future in the fight against cancer will be promising.

NASCAR Winston Racing Series Awards Banquet November 1994

(Note: Bill Jr. liked his politics more often than not on the conservative side. The 1994 awards banquet for NASCAR's grass-roots competition level, the NASCAR Winston Racing Series, was held just several days before Election Day. And so a keynote address that started out all about stock car racing took a quick, pro-Republican detour midway through. Read on.)

How big has the NASCAR Winston Racing series become? Well, the awards being distributed this year surpass three-quarters of a million dollars for the first time. That's big bucks.

Big bucks can sometimes breed big bureaucracy. Our industry is facing a huge tax-and-spend bureaucracy in Washington that seems to grow daily. There's an awful lot of politicians in Washington right now trying to get into your pockets every day. With that in mind, I urge you to vote Tuesday and send a message that you don't need more regulation, higher taxes, or a bunch of new hoops to jump through while trying to operate your business. You are the foundation, the solid rock of NASCAR. We're doing everything we can to move our business ahead despite the bureaucrats, but you need to be involved.

Rusty Wallace Retirement Announcement Daytona International Speedway August 2004

Today is without doubt bittersweet, as we're here to recognize Rusty Wallace for his great accomplishments in racing but at the same time start the process of saying so long.

From my perspective, it's nice to know he'll still be around, even if he's not in a race car.

Personally, I'd like to have Rusty around as long as possible, in whatever capacity possible. All of us at NASCAR have grown pretty accustomed to him—despite all the times he's given us hell about one thing or another.

NASCAR and Rusty Wallace haven't always agreed, which isn't exactly a secret.

But that's always been okay in my opinion, because the bottom line with Rusty is he's always been a team player when it comes right down to it.

Whatever his feelings on a particular issue, Rusty has always been interested in the betterment of the sport, and you certainly can't fault that.

I'll always remember him as a driver who helped boost NASCAR's popularity over the last 20 years. Rusty Wallace deserves a lot of credit for the success we're all experiencing today.

Rusty, it's been a pleasure to call you a NASCAR driver. It's been even more of a pleasure to call you my friend.

Daytona Beach Young Professionals Association
Daytona Beach International Airport
September 2005

Good afternoon.... It's nice to see so many bright, young, energetic people all together like this in one room. It speaks well for our community overall, but it especially speaks well for our business community's current state— and its future.

We're in pretty good hands right now where my office is, thanks to a couple of bright, young people who are leading the way at NASCAR and ISC.

Of course, I'm a little bit biased, since those people are also my kids, Brian and Lesa.

Motorsports Hall of Fame of America Induction
Novi, Michigan
July 2004

Tonight isn't really so much about me but about my family.

It's about the pride that comes from making something from nothing, which is just what my parents—Bill Sr. and Annie B. France—did more than 50 years ago when they founded NASCAR.

It's about the pride that comes from seeing your parents' dreams regarding NASCAR's growth come to fruition and knowing you played a part in that.

And it's about the pride that comes from seeing your children grow up into fine people who are ready to step in and keep the ball rolling, so to speak.

Of course, when I talk about family, I can't only talk about the France family. I also have to talk about the NASCAR Family, a clan that is nationwide but still close-knit.

As you might imagine, I'm pretty proud of that family, too.

Whenever one of these awards or honors comes my way, that sort of pride keeps me grounded by the perspective it provides.

I'm a lucky man.

I have two families.

One is made up of loving relatives—none more so than my wife, Betty Jane.

The other family consists of lasting friends.

Without those two families, I know I wouldn't be standing here tonight. Thank you.

Madison Avenue Sports Car & Chowder Society
New York City
January 1984

I guess you can mark your calendars. This is the first time I've devoted a talk to sports car racing, but I'm planning to do it a lot more in years to come.

The International Speedway Corporation and Corning Enterprises in Corning, New York, are partners in a venture at a race track called Watkins Glen International. This is one of the most exciting and challenging projects our sport has known. It's sort of like sending a favorite aunt in for a face lift. You don't want to see the good parts hurt, and you know it's bound to improve the old gal. We look at the Glen sort like a favorite aunt.

All-Sports Banquet
Elmira, New York
January 1984

As I look out over this audience and see so many fine young people, I get a little touch of sadness. It seems that almost from birth, youngsters are given a ball, a racket, a golf club, or any one of the other implements made for playing the stick-and-ball sports, as we call them. The youngsters get to hone their skills and become familiar with a chosen sport long before there is an opportunity to become a professional. In our sport of auto racing, we don't have that luxury. In most states, you have to be 16 before you can start driving a car, so that sort of puts us 16 years behind the other sports...

But there have to be reasons for auto racing's popularity, and I think I know at least part of the answer. First, it's basically non-stop action. Secondly, it is the one sport that blends the best points of athletic skill and the best points of technology...

A race car driver is a superb athlete with powers of concentration that are enormous.

Chapter Twenty-Four

Media

NASCAR's courtship of the media that began with Bill France Sr. blossomed into a full-fledged romance under Bill Jr.'s leadership. And, like any romance, it had its ups, downs, and plenty of both, perhaps because of Bill Jr.'s visibility on a weekly basis at the race track, which put him "out there" for better or worse.

Like his father, Bill Jr. understood the importance of the media to the business of NASCAR. Here's what he told the Associated Press Sports Editors' national convention in 1998 in Richmond, Virginia, when he was the annual event's keynote speaker.

"We are convinced that our customers are your customers," he said, talking to a large group of sports media decision-makers, a group that was probably a mostly skeptical bunch despite NASCAR's then-burgeoning popularity. Bill Jr. had a firm grasp of that skepticism that day, telling the editors, "I want to try and give you a glimpse of what is really going on in the world of NASCAR, a world that I suspect may be as foreign to you as a trip to Mars…. The fact is, we at NASCAR have a clear idea of who we are, where we're headed, and what's fueling our success. Unlike the actual races we hold, our organization isn't running in circles and only turning left. NASCAR is the fastest-growing sport in the country, and I'm proud of what we've accomplished."

From there, Bill Jr. launched into a half-hour speech that was really more of a lecture aimed at educating his audience about the viability of NASCAR as a mainstream sport. He spoke at length about skills required to be a NASCAR driver, dismissing the notion that drivers aren't athletes. He wanted those editors to walk out of that room with at least a tad more respect for people like Dale Earnhardt and Jeff Gordon.

In recognition of his audience consisting of sports editors from across the nation, he supplied a national perspective, addressing the stereotype of NASCAR fans being solely from the Southeast. "NASCAR fans are hard to put a label on," he said. "They're young and old...male and female...affluent and modest...from big cities and small towns...they're from the North, South, East, and West, a true cross-section of America.

"Now, I realize most of you didn't grow up with NASCAR racing. The sports of your youth were probably played with bats and balls, hoops or pigskins, when NASCAR wasn't an ingrained part of the landscape of American pastimes. But now it is. And as our popularity grows, so will the interest of your readers. As I said before, NASCAR fans are your fans."

He closed with one of his favorite stories about NASCAR's relationship with the media, a tale dating to 1948 when Big Bill France was trying to get his arms around his dream of a national-level stock-car body. The story goes that Big Bill went to visit the sports editor of the *Charlotte Observer*, Wilt Garrison, to pitch a story about NASCAR's first national championship. Garrison supposedly expressed doubts about the credibility of the "national" label since the races and victories were relatively few. Garrison suggested an extensive series with a true accumulation of points reflective of the schedule, along the lines of other sports' statistics and standings.

"My father," Bill Jr. told the sports editors, "knew a good idea when he heard it, so he said thanks and soon the NASCAR Strictly Stock Series was born. I guess you can say that in a way, the print media is partially responsible for legitimizing our sport.

"And I dare say your attention now can contribute to our future growth."

Ten years later, in Minneapolis, Minnesota, Brian France addressed the APSE convention and referenced his father's speech—and his feelings about the media.

"Despite my father's reputation for being a little contentious at times, he actually liked the media, especially the writers—although he sometimes did a good job hiding it," Brian said. "He absolutely loved sparring with the writers."

One of Bill Jr.'s old sparring partners concurred.

"I think there was a time when it was fair to say he was as accessible to the media—or more so—as any head of a major sport," said Al Pearce, the longtime auto racing writer at the *Newport News (Virginia) Press*. "I don't think former NFL commissioner Pete Rozelle made himself as accessible to the media as Bill Jr. did. I don't think the various MLB commissioners through the years picked up the phone and called reporters back—which Bill Jr. did as a matter of course. All I know is that whenever I needed Bill for anything, I'd call down to Daytona and he'd either call me right back or his office would put him right on the phone.

"In my mind, one of his great strengths was that he was always willing to listen to people in the media, their suggestions, what they thought. Now, he might not always agree with you of course; sometimes he would ask one of us, 'What do you think?' And we'd come back with, 'Gee, Mr. France, I dunno, it's your company.' But then he'd come right back and say again, 'Yeah, but what do you think?'

"I feel like that really said a lot about him, that he listened to us. And he would do this sort of thing every week in the media center—just sit there and bullshit with you. And he was not above asking a weekly newspaper reporter or a small-daily outlet guy like me what they thought about something. I don't know if any other major sports leader interacted with media like that. It was always refreshing."

One particular interaction sticks with Pearce to this day. It illustrates the mixture of pragmatism and humor Bill France Jr. displayed while running his sport.

"The best story I have about him happened on the Tuesday after the 1979 Daytona 500," Pearce began, a smile widening. "That was two days after one of the most famous races in NASCAR history, one ended by a three-driver brawl involving Bobby Allison, his brother Donnie, and Cale Yarborough after a Turn 3 accident. While those guys fought, Richard Petty cruised by to take the victory."

It was electric—and it was watched by millions. For the first time, the 500 was broadcast flag to flag on CBS. Race day coincided with a massive winter storm throughout the Northeast, leaving many of the nation's most-populated areas virtually snowbound. Meaning people were indoors, and many were watching television. The captive audience of sorts was treated to classic stock-car theatre. Ratings were huge.

"So," Pearce continued, "I asked Bill Jr. if he's planning to fine any of the drivers involved in the fight. I'll never forget that here came this big booming voice into phone: 'Fine? Fine? What do you mean, fine? I should give them a bonus. You can't buy that kind of publicity.'"

Pearce has another story of a different time, nearly 30 years later. Bill Jr., his health failing, was at the Waldorf Astoria Hotel in New York City for the annual NASCAR Sprint Cup Series Awards Ceremony. Spotted in the lobby, he agreed to an impromptu interview, carefully answering questions about a touchy subject—the possibility of NASCAR ending its relationship with the Waldorf—a relationship that dated to 1981 when Bill Jr. moved the season-ending awards show from Daytona Beach to the famed hotel.

"He was even accessible in that situation, within the parameters his endurance would allow," Pearce said. "I don't think he ever blew off a media member's questions, as long as they were legitimate and not some smart-ass deal.

"I just thought Bill France Jr. was a terrific guy."

These observations by Pearce, colored by a noticeable and considerable affection for Bill Jr., contrast somewhat with the image of the tough-talking, hard-ass ruler. Pearce's point is that while Bill Jr. was strident at times, his firm decisions followed considerable conversation and debate—both within and outside the confines of NASCAR's offices, including much discourse with the media, who seldom passed up a chance to disagree with how NASCAR was being run.

Even former *Winston-Salem Journal* reporter Mike Mulhern displays an obvious affection for Bill Jr. The reason this is worth noting is that Mulhern was, as Geri McMullin laughingly reminds, "always a pain in Bill Jr.'s ass."

"Bill Jr. was fun," Mulhern said of his former adversary. Mulhern, whose work now appears on his own Web site, covered NASCAR for years for the *Journal*—the same city where R.J. Reynolds headquarters is located. Mulhern's coverage was comprehensive and controversial; always on the scene and prowling the garage area, he was renowned for taking chances when it came to breaking stories and the citing of "NASCAR sources" to back things up.

Sometimes Mulhern scored. Sometimes he landed considerably off the mark. Like the time back in July 1997 during the summer racing weekend at Daytona when NASCAR scheduled a morning press conference. Rumors circulated about potential topics, one being a possible retirement announcement by Bill Jr. Mulhern reported in the *Journal* that would indeed be the subject of the gathering, and that the 35-year-old Brian France, NASCAR's director of marketing, would replace his father as the organization's president.

Next morning, an eager crowd of media convened in a tent outside the main grandstand, where it was announced that Daytona International Speedway would be installing a state-of-the-art lighting system in time for the next year's summertime event.

Mulhern had whiffed again but that never has stopped him—or his audience. Throughout his career he has been read extensively, and he was especially read by Bill France Jr., who had longtime ties to the Winston-Salem area.

"Bill Jr. would always be in your face, but you could always be in his face about…whatever," Mulhern said. "He was always there at the race track.

"He had that big yellow magic marker, and if you wrote something he didn't like, which I did every now and then—probably a little more than now and then—he would call you into the NASCAR hauler, kick everybody else out and throw a copy of your paper down on the table. There'd be all sorts of yellow marks all over your story. You'd have to explain what you meant about everything. But it was good. You got some feedback, you know?"

You also got some needling. There was a time when Mulhern, always the eccentric, decided he would try to supplement the wire services' photography offerings by taking some pictures himself, and he was often seen snapping away with a 35mm camera. Bill Jr. jumped on this opportunity, giving Mulhern the nickname "paparazzi." Only he pronounced it "paparatchi." He used to ask other media members, "You guys seen paparatchi around today?"

NASCAR vice president Jim Hunter is an old newspaperman, a former sportswriter at the *Atlanta Journal-Constitution*. "Bill Jr. had a love-hate relationship with Mulhern," Hunter said. "He definitely didn't like a lot about [what] Mulhern wrote because he was in the hometown of our sponsor, and Mulhern was always bashing NASCAR."

No love existed in the relationship between Bill Jr. and the late Gene Granger, a newspaper reporter in Spartanburg, South Carolina, and other local papers who later became a freelance writer and statistician for NASCAR's major sponsor R.J. Reynolds. "Granger was always writing that Bill Jr. was a crook, a liar, and just terrible stuff," Hunter said. "Bill would never comment publicly about what Granger wrote, but he used to ask me how a guy could get away with writing things like that, wondering why his editors allowed it."

Bill Jr.'s widow, Betty Jane France, remembers she would read something negative about NASCAR and get "a lot more upset about than Bill would. He would always tell me the media was just doing their job. He would never write a letter to the editor or anything like that. I guess he would do things like what Mulhern describes, more in private with the media. The yellow marker, that sounds like Bill for sure."

Hunter has a funny story, sort of. "One year, during a time when the press was really busting NASCAR's ass about something, Bill Jr. came into the media

142

center and told the writers that they needed to remember that if it wasn't for NASCAR, they wouldn't have jobs. Yeah, that's what he actually told them. Then he told them, 'NASCAR is your Sugar Daddy.'"

A week later, Bill Jr. had his public relations person passing out actual Sugar Daddys in the media center to soothe things over. "Bill Jr. was going around asking the reporters 'Did you get my Sugar Daddy?'" Hunter said.

In his later years, as the Internet expanded and made an unbelievable amount of media coverage instantly accessible around the clock, Bill Jr. was in his glory. He became fond of pre-dawn perusing of newspaper Web sites, which meant that early-morning phone calls to employees to discuss that day's coverage became commonplace.

NASCAR's former chief operations officer, George Pyne, tells a story about boarding a NASCAR company plane one morning in Daytona Beach for a flight to Charlotte. Pyne was still in the process of strapping his 6'5" frame into his seat when Bill Jr. was all over him, quizzing him about a particular story published that day that was less than complimentary about NASCAR. Pyne said he had yet to read the daily clip report provided to NASCAR executives.

"Here, let me save you some time," Bill Jr. said, tossing a stack of print-outs into Pyne's lap. The then-70-year-old chairman and CEO of NASCAR had assembled his own damn clip report, probably around 7:00 AM on this particular morning, and he relished beating his young executive to the punch.

Bill Jr. used the Internet to prepare for interviews, painstakingly researching a writer's past stories about NASCAR. He also researched the writer. In 2005, a freelancer who worked regularly for one of the country's leading newspapers came to Bill Jr.'s office for an interview. Before the first question was asked, the old man set the tone.

"Now, let me understand something…you're just a stringer, right?" he said, referring to the print business jargon for a freelancer.

"Yes, that's right," the writer responded half-heartedly.

"I guess he just wanted to establish the upper hand right off the bat," the writer said later.

Which he indeed had done.

Mulhern and Granger aside, when you consider a career-long body of work, the title of the most truly adversarial media member for Bill Jr. may well belong to

Ed Hinton, who has covered motorsports for a variety of publications, including the *Atlanta Journal-Constitution, Sports Illustrated, The National* (a short-lived, high-quality daily sports magazine in the 1990s), the Tribune Company (*Los Angeles Times, Chicago Tribune,* and *Orlando Sentinel* are some of the papers in that chain), and currently ESPN.com.

Hinton achieved notoriety beyond his considerable journalistic skills in 1999 ironically *because* of those skills. Hinton wrote a piece for *Sports Illustrated* about an Indy Racing League event's accident that resulted in the deaths of three spectators. The story was accompanied by a photograph of a victim's body covered by a sheet. Writers do not make the decisions on photography for their stories, but that didn't stop Indianapolis Motor Speedway and the IRL from denying Hinton a credential to cover that year's Indianapolis 500. In response, the *Chicago Tribune* announced it would boycott the 500 not so much in support of its future employee but rather as a response against "censorship" by the IRL. Soon after, the IRL relented.

Hinton, who apparently never met a controversy he couldn't become identified with, was thrust into the national spotlight again when Earnhardt was killed due to his week-long "racing safety" series that was published in the days leading up to the Daytona 500. He became the designated media "expert" on safety after the accident. Unwittingly, he also came to be the face of the media's attempts to gain access to the Earnhardt autopsy photos, which he had nothing to do with.

During his many years of writing about NASCAR, Hinton has become renowned for developing sources—and agitating those sources, all the while writing some of the most masterful pieces you can find on the sport of stock car racing or auto racing in general. His captivating and comprehensive 2001 book, *Daytona,* is a testament to his talents, a history of racing in Daytona Beach that concludes with the 2001 event.

Hinton's longtime working relationship with Bill France Jr. was damaged considerably in 2001, to the point where the requisite interviews when needed were no longer assured. It took several years for the two to start talking again. The fact that they did start is all the proof anyone will ever need to show how important the media was in Bill Jr.'s opinion.

In February 2004, Bill Jr. held court in the Daytona infield media center. Hinton was front and center at the small table. Bill Jr. was "dancing with the devil" again, the joke went. They danced that day long after the other reporters had left, their conversation more a mutual reminiscing between two old war horses than an interview.

Hinton half-expected the iciness to thaw between himself and Bill Jr. He had seen a glimpse of the old live-and-let-live days from two years before.

"I was leaving the old credential building that was right over by the NASCAR offices," Hinton said. "I had just picked up my Daytona 500 credentials. I was walking out of the building and about to step off the curb when I looked up and saw this SUV coming at quite a clip. I stopped myself, but then all of a sudden the SUV stopped short of where I was and the driver was waving me to go on across.

"It was Bill Jr.

"As I was crossing the street, he rolled down his window and yelled, 'I want you to know that a year ago, I would've run over your ass.'

"That was Bill Jr.—and that was his way of saying that all was well, that everything was water under the bridge at that point."

It was another example of Bill Jr.'s pragmatism.

"Bill Jr.," Hunter said, "was always very cognizant of the role the media played in getting the NASCAR story out to the world."

Chapter Twenty-Five

Stories

When the idea of a book about the life of Bill France Jr. was first being considered, NASCAR senior vice president Paul Brooks, a man who grew very close to Bill Jr. during his later years, asked people throughout the NASCAR industry for special remembrances or stories to share. The collective response was gratifying as the tales poured in; everyone who was asked, it seemed, had been touched by Bill Jr. in one way or another. Some contributions were of a personal nature—both hilarious and serious. Some were glowing tributes. Others came across as acknowledgments of Bill Jr.'s business acumen.

The point being, of course, that the contributions came more than a year after his death. The words provided were vivid, as if the memories were from only a few days in the past rather than years ago.

Portions of the various submissions appear throughout this book, fitting into a particular time period or development in Bill Jr.'s life. A number of submissions are somewhat timeless, random—but still essential to understanding the man, especially those more personal in tone.

A sampling of those submissions follow, starting off with a couple of classics that are well known among NASCAR employees, as told by Bill Jr.'s son, the present chairman and CEO of NASCAR, Brian France.

Brian France, NASCAR Chairman and CEO

"This was some years back, leading up to Christmas, probably the 23rd of December. It was in the afternoon and my dad was gone for the day—or rather, I *thought* he was gone.

"His car was gone from out front of our building. What I didn't know was that he was in the process of changing cars at the time, so another car was out front that I didn't know he was driving. So I didn't think he was in the office.

"A few days beforehand, I'd asked him about letting our people go home early for the holiday. He had denied that request. Didn't think that was a good idea. Well, when I thought he was gone...

"At that time, you could speak over the building PA system from your telephone. So I got on the PA and gave everybody the rest of the day off. Unbeknownst [to me], he was sitting at his desk and heard it.

"He immediately got on his own phone and canceled what I thought was a good idea. And everybody heard it."

"My dad called me out in Los Angeles when 9/11 happened. He said that he recognized the extent of the tragedy but that he saw it was isolated down in Lower Manhattan.

"We have a NASCAR office in Midtown Manhattan and he was trying to get a hold of somebody in that office. Of course, like everybody else, we had let our people go for the day.

"At that point, you couldn't drive in and out of the city. People were walking everywhere. The day after the tragedy, our people were out again. My dad called me again. He was still trying to reach someone in the New York office. He wanted to know why no one was in there.

"I asked him if he'd been watching the news. I told him that no one is in their offices in New York and furthermore you can't drive right now.

"He told me, 'Well, I see people walking across those bridges.'

"He thought that our people should be getting into work. He wanted them to walk to work. I explained to him that probably wasn't possible because we had people who lived in Connecticut and New Jersey, but anyway..."

John Cassidy, Long-Time NASCAR legal counsel

(Note: Bill France Jr. loved hot dogs. If people don't know it, they should. He always had them a special way, grilling the bun just right. We had a special place to go for hot dogs, Pulliams Hot Dog Stand in Winston-Salem, and he loved taking people there. Here's a great story told by John Cassidy, NASCAR's long-time legal counsel and Washington D.C. resident, about his first visit to Pulliams.)

"It was me, Bill France Sr., Bill Jr., and NASCAR's Jim Hunter, all flying together from Daytona. The three of them were going to New York I believe, and they were going to drop me off in Washington on the way. Well, at one point early in the flight Bill Sr. and Bill Jr. started pulling out these little handbooks they always carried with them in which they had written down information about great restaurants all over the country and the world. Bill Jr. announced that we had to stop off in Winston-Salem, because there was a great French restaurant we had to go to. He called it, 'Le Pull-yam.'

"Well, both he and his dad went on and on about this place so I said sure, let's go. Thing is, they said, this was a really nice place and you had to be somewhat dressed up, at least in a coat and tie. They were in coats and ties but I think I was in blue jeans.

"We land and it's pouring rain. But the car's waiting for us so I had to change my clothes, in the rain *under the airplane wing.* Really. That was some sight as you can imagine. Then, we also had to stop at a store so I could buy a tie.

"After that we drive off to 'Le Pull-yam.' Well, all of a sudden we pull up to this building that looks like a goddamn shack! It's a roadside hot dog stand! They get out to run in and I followed them. They start pointing to the place's sign, laughing.

"The sign read 'Pulliams.'

"They were good hot dogs, but I mean.... They really got me good. And it was quite some time before I found out that this joke was something they'd hatched a good while beforehand. They had this all set up. Billy and his father were constantly playing jokes on people like that.

"Yeah.... 'Le Pull-yam.'"

Robin Braig, Daytona International Speedway President
"Before I came to Daytona, I was at Phoenix International Raceway. One morning about 6:00 AM out there, Bill Jr. called me and woke me up. He obviously wasn't thinking about the time difference. I answered the phone and right away he was asking me, 'Have you heard about the spotted owl deal out there where you are?'

"It's 6:00 AM, I'm half asleep, and I don't know what the hell he's talking about. What had happened was a story had broken that morning about the spotted owl being an endangered species and a wide area of Arizona had been designated at the time as not being allowed to have any sort of construction. This was right when we were building a new grandstand at the speedway, so this wasn't good news for us.

"Bill had a solution, though. He told me to go down to the humane society and get a bunch of cats. Lots of them. Then he wanted me to take them out to the desert and let them go. 'You won't have a spotted owl problem anymore, I guarantee you that. You might have a cat problem, but no more spotted owl problem.'

"Of course he was kidding...I think."

"Back in 2005, after I'd become the president of Daytona International Speedway, Bill Jr. let me know that the famous NBC news anchor Tom Brokaw was coming to town along with his producer for a one-day visit to the race track. Brokaw and Bill had met some years earlier and had kept in touch through the years. This was a very big deal to Bill, a chance to show off his favorite track to one of the world's most famous journalists.

"The plan was to start the day by watching the NASCAR IMAX movie at our fan attraction, the Daytona 500 Experience. We then would go inside the track where the two newsmen would be driven around the speedway in stock cars, courtesy of the Richard Petty Driving Experience. We'd top it off with lunch inside the track, in the infield, old-fashioned picnic style.

"Well, we all met at the speedway that morning and went into the Experience's theatre to watch the movie. We settled into our seats—about eight of us. Bill Jr. was to the front and right of the group slightly. The movie started, ran for about 10 seconds and then shuddered to a stop, leaving us all in complete darkness. A few moments passed and it cranked up again, to my relief.

"But that relief was short-lived.

"This time, the movie flickered for only a second or two—then went kaput for good. So there we sat in a silent, blackened theatre: Bill France Jr., Tom Brokaw, Brokaw's producer, and a very nervous Daytona International Speedway president.

"Then came the voice: 'Goddammit, Robin!'

"Bill Jr. was pissed. Thankfully, his longtime friend and employee, NASCAR vice president Jim Hunter, was there as well. After Bill's comment, Hunter started to chuckle slightly. It wasn't much, but it helped to lighten the mood somewhat.

"So that was a great start to the day. Well, it got better. We loaded up into our cars and headed toward the infield and the track rides. Thing was, we were now about a half-hour ahead of schedule. So when we arrived in the garage area, anxious to put Brokaw and his producer into the cars, especially after the movie debacle…the damn cars weren't ready yet! This made Bill Jr. even more agitated, as you can imagine.

"With the mechanics thrashing away to get the cars set and the Petty Driving Experience people scurrying around to get the fire suits for our guests, Bill Jr. came walking straight toward me. The look on his face was not pleasant. He got right in my face and told me, 'Well Braig, I guess that job at Nazareth Speedway is looking pretty good to you right about now, isn't it?'

"International Speedway Corporation was getting close to closing Nazareth at the time. So Bill's words weren't exactly comforting.

"Nonetheless, we persevered. We got them into the cars, they had great fun riding around the track, and we had a wonderful cookout lunch where Brokaw regaled us all with some great stories about his career.

"We then went back to see the movie and that time, it worked. At the end of the day, everything has worked out fine.

"Sort of.

"Bill never let me forget about the miscues—or how close I came to working at Nazareth.

"Of course he was kidding…I think."

Jim "Bocky" Bockoven, former NASCAR official and lifelong friend

"I knew Billy from back in the fourth grade, around 1941. I lived on Halifax off one side of Main Street, and he lived on Goodall over on the other side of Main. Down by his house there was, like, a circle where you went in, hit a dead end, and came back out. One day we heard Billy was going to put on a bicycle race on that circle. So four or five of us from Seabreeze Elementary went over to Billy's house and signed up. The entry fee was $1.

"Well, the day of the race it rained all day. We never ran. So after that, we'd see Billy and ask when he was gonna reschedule the race. He'd say, 'Down the road.' He never did reschedule—and we never got our money back.

"Typical promoter."

"Billy went to Lenox Elementary in Daytona Beach, and I went to Seabreeze Elementary. Then we both went to Seabreeze High School. Billy, well, he wasn't much of a high school athlete. He was, oh, kind of clumsy. But he played basketball anyway, on what they called the 'B' squad. They played their games before the 'A' squad games, and Billy got to play a little bit. I don't think Billy ever dressed for an 'A' squad game.

"The coach at the time, Joe Nelson, had a rule that if you were a senior and you didn't make the 'first six,' you got cut. We had pretty good teams back then; we won four straight state titles (1948–51). Senior year, Billy got cut. But so did some other guys who had played on championship teams and were walking around with the championship letter jackets.

"It was a couple years later after we graduated and both of us were home from the navy. Seabreeze was having a Christmas tournament, so we decided to go see a game one night. Well, that season, Coach Nelson didn't have a very good team at all. We sat right behind the bench. Seabreeze was losing pretty bad, and Billy reached over and tapped Coach on the shoulder and said, 'Hey, don't you wish you had me now?'

"Coach Nelson was so damned mad at him. He said, 'Get outta here, France.'

"Billy...he was somethin'."

Gary Smith, NASCAR Director of Event Logistics

"I first met Bill France Jr. in the spring of 1991. I was running boats for a living at the time, and Tommy Callahan, who ran the marine department for NASCAR, called me and asked if I would come to Daytona and interview for an opening they had for their summer trip that year. I had just left a job running boats for a family for 13 years and was freelancing at the time, so this opportunity seemed worth checking out.

"I had never met Bill before, and during the interview process he came across as very gruff and grumpy.

"I liked him immediately.

"I was hired to do a short trip to the Bahamas to see if I would fit in, and thus started a 16-year relationship with the finest man I have ever known.

"It didn't take long to figure out three things that Bill loved in this world. First and foremost was his family. His wife Betty Jane was as much a part of his life as the air he breathed...he doted on her always. His children, Brian and Lesa, were the constant subjects of his bragging, and his pride in them and their accomplishments was always very clear to me. His brother Jim and his son-in-law Bruce Kennedy also were obviously quite special to him, as well.

"The second thing that was evident to me was that Bill loved NASCAR. It was not just the family business but a way of life to Bill. It seemed that you couldn't separate Bill from NASCAR. When that man got up in the morning he was NASCAR, and when he went to bed at night he was NASCAR, and most of the time in between he was NASCAR. He absolutely loved what he did for a living like no one else I have ever met.

"The third thing that Bill seemed to really like was fishing. I had been an offshore fisherman for a large part of my life, but I had never met a man with more passion for it than Bill.

"The species of saltwater fish that Bill targeted wasn't what most offshore anglers went after. He would 'tolerate' trolling for billfish or other pelagic species, but what really got him excited was bottom fishing—specifically bottom fishing for Yellow Eye Snapper. Over the years we would travel to almost every island, rock, and ledge in the Bahamas in search of good yellow eye spots.

"The only other fishing that Bill really liked was fishing in any kind of private impromptu tournament he and his pals could put together. Keep in mind that these 'tournaments' were not necessarily contests of skill but more to stir up controversy and laughter than anything else.

"Here's a classic: Once, in the summer of '91, we were fishing in one of these mini-tournaments at Cat Cay in the Bahamas. It was just a one-day affair put together for entertainment, and it was decided that the biggest fish of any kind would win. Well, the fishing was as slow as it gets during the summer doldrums when Bill spotted an old Bahamian fisherman checking his traps. Instructing us to pull up to the old gentleman's skiff, Bill proceeded to barter with him for his catch. Unfortunately all the fellow had was a grouper that had been in the trap too long and was getting close to rotting. Nevertheless, a short while later a very happy old Bahamian left with cash, beer, and a new hat, and we left with a half-rotten fish and headed back to the dock.

"At the weigh-in, the grouper was found to be the biggest fish of the day and our team was ready to receive our accolades when an astute member of the other team noticed that flies were all swarming on our one big fish, ignoring the other fish on the dock. Well, of course Bill confessed to our ruse, and an annual competition of not just fishing but deception and good laughs was born.

"Later on through the years, if a situation in business was questionable and you ever heard Bill ask if the deal would pass the 'fly test,' that's where the term came from.

"I learned a lot from being around Bill…he was a unique individual. I thought the world of that man, and I always will."

Felix Sabates, NASCAR Sprint Cup Series team owner

"Bill and I were out fishing one time, way the hell out in the middle of nowhere. This was back when satellite dishes were first coming out, and I had a big dish on my boat. Another boat was going to bring a bunch of other guys out to meet us the next day, but this was a Sunday, just me and Bill, watching a Darlington race.

"Bill had a satellite phone on the floor next to him, which was hooked up live to the NASCAR tower. So we're watching the race and Geoff Bodine comes in to pit. When he leaves, he runs over the air hose, but the official misses it. Bill had just seen it, so he picks up the phone and calls the tower. He told them, 'You need to black flag that boy because he just ran over the hose.' And they did. Bill Jr. called that penalty from 1,000 miles away."

Rusty Wallace, 1989 NASCAR Sprint Cup Series champion

"It was back in 1993…I won 10 races that year. I was just winnin' [the] hell out of everything, but while I was winnin' I thought I was still at a disadvantage because my Pontiac had a shorter deck lid than everybody else. When we took the car to the wind tunnel, the data always showed that the car wasn't as good as the competition.

"So we took all this data to Bill Jr. We had all these reasons why we were at a disadvantage down on paper to show him. I'll never forget, we bring him all the info and he says to me, 'Let me tell you what: I don't give a crap about all this paper. All I have to do is sit up in the tower, look down, and watch you go around the track and watch everybody else go around. And I don't care if you're at a disadvantage or not. This year, you don't need nothing.

"He was so straight-forward. Now get this: The next year I switched to Fords. Well, as soon as I announced I was switching to Fords from Pontiacs, he gave Pontiacs a 2-inch longer deck lid."

"Darlington, South Carolina…I hear someone beating on my motor-home door. This was on a Monday after we'd had a rainout on a Sunday. The way I heard it, Bill Jr. was sitting in the NASCAR hauler with a bunch of drivers and crew chiefs when all of a sudden he said, 'Today's April Fools' Day. Let's play a joke on somebody. Who should it be? Wait, I know: Wallace, 'cause that sonofabitch will go completely nuts if we play a joke on him.'

"He got with track security and told them to go tell me that Bill France Jr. wanted to see me right then. So here security came, beating my door down.

"I went over to the hauler and Bill Jr. says, 'Where were you after the drivers' meeting?' I asked him what he was talking about and told him that I'd gone to the drivers' meeting on Sunday. He says, 'That was yesterday and there was a rainout, so we had another drivers' meeting.' I told him that was a bunch of bullshit, because we'd never had a second drivers' meeting after a rainout in the history of our sport. He comes right back and says, 'Well, we changed the rules, you didn't show for the meeting, so now you're going to start at the back of the field.'

"I had qualified fourth, so I was all jacked up about the race. I saw red. I was so damn mad I couldn't breathe. I got a cup of coffee and sat down. After awhile I told him, 'Mr. France, you act like you don't even care.' He says, 'Let me tell you something: I don't give a shit. You're starting at the back.'

"Well, I slung that cup of coffee against the wall of that hauler and said, 'Okay you m— f—, if that's the way you want it, you're gonna see a rocket come up from the back to the front.' Right after I threw the coffee, everybody in the hauler burst out laughing. Bill Jr. about fell off his chair.

"Then he looked at me and said, 'I knew you'd go crazy…. April Fools, asshole.'"

"One year I remember I had gone over to Bill Jr.'s office in Daytona Beach—just messing around for awhile because it was before practice and I had some time to go visit with him. We were sitting there talking, and he told me I was running good at the time. Then he told me this:

'Wallace, what I see, watching your performance through the years, is a career going up, up, up, and is now at a peak.'

154

"To illustrate that, he held one hand out flat, then placed that hand atop the fingers of his other hand, then rocked the top hand back and forth, showing me that he thought my career was teetering a little bit, maybe starting to go down. At the time, I think I'd gone from winning 10 races one year, then down to five wins, then down to one win, stuff like that. He asked me about retiring, saying, 'How much longer are you going to keep doing this? There are a lot of other cool things you can do in this sport. You've done everything you can, won a championship, etc.'

"Well, in February 2001, Dale Earnhardt dies. My wife and I, we run over to the hospital after the Daytona 500 and right away we see Bill Jr. there. He says, 'Man, he passed away,' or something like that.

"He walked away down the hall, then turned around. I was looking at Bill Jr. from a distance at that point. He looked at me and just shook his head. And then he held up his hands, putting them together like he had that time in his office years earlier, rocking the top hand. It was like he was asking me again: 'Do you really want to keep racing?'

"That was the most emotional moment I ever remember personally about Bill France Jr."

Humpy Wheeler, former president of Charlotte Motor Speedway

"I was the showman; he was the realist. I was the one who liked to take things to the edge of the cliff; he would try to pull me back. I can remember that voice, yelling at me more than once, saying, 'What are you doing? That's nuts!'

"Negotiating with him was a real challenge and sometimes fun. He was a great negotiator, dead-panned, never showing his hand. He became very stoic when the cards were on the table and had great endurance.

"Sometimes we were at great odds. Once I went down to Daytona Beach to negotiate with him and Les Richter over a TV deal.

"We negotiated—arguing mostly—for seven straight hours without a bathroom break. I looked at Les Richter and said, 'Does he ever go to the bathroom?' Richter said, 'Not until the issue was solved.' I finally gave in and hit the john."

"Bill invited me and the late T. Wayne Robertson of R.J. Reynolds to go fishing down in Palm Beach, Florida, one July. We went out in a 19-foot center console about three miles off the beach. A terrible thunderstorm began bearing down on us from the West, where streaks of lightning looked ominous.

"Like most old-time track operators, I pride myself in weather forecasting and said to Bill, 'We need to get the hell out of here before we get hit. That's nasty.' He said, 'Don't worry. It'll die when it hits the beach.' Well, those things don't do that in the Carolinas, I told him. He calmly went on fishing as the sky turned black and big boomers rang through the sky.

"I sat there and wondered when the lightning was going to hit our tiny boat. Ten minutes later the blackness hit the beach and, just as he predicted, it simply died and everything cleared.

"He looked at me and said, 'Someday you'll start listening to me.'"

"When anything really bad happened, we usually talked. Things like a driver's death or something else going wrong at a track of his, mine, or anyone's. He always wanted to know if the problem that led to the mishap could be permanently fixed.

"When Bobby Allison almost got into the grandstand at Talladega, we talked for a long time about that. When three spectators were killed at Charlotte at an Indy-car race, I called him and we talked forever. A promoter's life can sometimes be very lonely. Who can you talk with about a problem? How many of us are there? Bill was always there to talk."

Rick Hendrick, owner, Hendrick Motorsports

"I was scared to death of Bill when I first met him. I remember going into the NASCAR hauler one day at a race track with Larry McClure. We had been complaining about NASCAR taking our cars to the wind tunnel to check them out.

"Bill was sitting inside the hauler. Larry walked in and said something like, 'Bill, I don't think I want you to take my car to the wind tunnel.' Bill looked at him and said, 'I *will* take your goddamn car to the wind tunnel, and if you don't like it, there's the gate. You can leave, and don't come back.'

"Then Bill turned to me and said, 'Now, what do you want, Rick?'

"I said, 'Oh, nothing...I just came by to say hello.'"

"I remember this one day at Talladega. Chuck Rider, Felix Sabates, and I were standing around together and Bill walked by. Chuck Rider said to Bill, 'You know, the tracks are making money, the drivers are making money, but the car owners are suffering. We need you to do something to help out the car owners.'

"Bill looked at Chuck and said, 'Let me tell you something. I don't need you.'

"Then he looked at Felix and said, 'I don't need you.'

"Then he looked at me and said, 'And I don't need you.... All I need is somebody to pay. Did anybody ever tell you [that you] were going to get rich by being a car owner?'

"Then he just turned around and walked off. One thing I learned early on about Bill France Jr. was that you always needed to get him one on one. You never wanted to approach him in a crowd to complain about something. One-on-one, you had a shot. But in a crowd, he was going to defend NASCAR and defend his position—and trash your ass in front of people!"

Edsel Ford II, Ford board of directors

"I truly treasured my relationship with Bill France over the years, but even I wasn't immune to getting at least one call to visit the NASCAR trailer to meet with him when he had something he wanted to get across to us.

"My favorite memories of Bill, however, will always be when he would host a small dinner for some of us on his boat in Miami when I first was grand marshal of the Ford Championship Weekend in Homestead, Florida. He was a great host. I think I learned more about NASCAR and his vision for the sport in those few dinners than I ever could have learned anywhere else. He would tell us great stories about the early days of NASCAR and about his father. We got great insight into the decision-making process that helped him take the sport where he thought it should go.

"In many ways he was very similar to my father, Henry Ford II. Both of them were asked to take the reins of their companies at a fairly young age, and they both had great vision for the future of their companies. That vision helped them take Ford Motor Company and NASCAR successfully into a new era. I miss Bill to this day, and I miss my conversations with him."

Raymond Mason Jr., board of directors, International Speedway Corporation

"With racing, it all started for me when I climbed out of the back seat of my neighbor's sports car. As I looked around the race track known as Daytona International Speedway, I was filled with the wonder and amazement of a 13-year-old boy and had no idea where this new experience would take me. I knew one thing for sure—in that instant, I was hooked on racing.

"A few years later I had the opportunity to meet the France family, and for more than 20 years, I had an inside look at the life of an incredible man and important figure in racing, Bill France Jr. I was always amazed by his down-to-earth and no-nonsense nature, and throughout the years, my respect and admiration for him never wavered. Bill was a man you could count on; a man who said what he meant and meant what he said. A son a father could be proud of.

"As a steward of America's racing legacy, he took NASCAR above and beyond the dreams of his father. I remember a particular conversation of few words we had some years ago with great fondness. It was the first night race held at Daytona International Speedway, October 1998; it was a night to remember. As the glow of the newly installed lights began to fill the crisp fall air, the pre-race excitement of the crowd was clearly evident, and thousands of camera flashes punctuated the night sky like a swarm of fireflies in the background. The race cars lined up on the track took on a sparkle under the new lights, and I knew everyone there felt how special this night was.

"I was taking a second bite of my hot dog when Bill France Jr. sat down beside me and asked me, 'Raymond, what do you think Dad would have thought of this?' I patted him on his shoulder and said, 'Your dad would be mighty proud.'

"His father had once told me that 'Bill knows racing.' There was no daylight burned that evening as Bill France Jr. went about the business he knew so well—racing. It was a magical night, and it made for a magical memory."

Ken Clapp, former director of the NASCAR West Series

"This one goes back more than 35 years ago. I had just gotten married again, and my wife and I were on our honeymoon in the Carmel, California, area where there was an event going on in what was, back then, called the Winston West Series. I hadn't seen Bill in more than a year. Betty Jane was with him. We ran into them at the event inspection, which was at a Macy's Department Store garage on a Friday.

"He asked, 'Where you eatin' tonight? We ought to eat together.' So we did, and the wives hit it off well. The next day, they took off in one rental car and me and Bill took off in another rental car, headed toward the race track.

"We get almost to the track and there was a perimeter road outside the place. A dirt perimeter road, I might add. Bill said it looked like we could get from 'here to there' using the road. I told him I wasn't sure about that because there was a gully separating the perimeter road from the track. He said, 'Nah, we'll straddle that thing.'

"So we headed down the dirt road [and] all of a sudden we started losing our grip. We got sideways, and then we turned it over. In the process of doing that, we hooked a chain-link fence and rolled about 50 feet of it up, as if we had planned it, as we were sliding and rolling. We stopped and all this fence is on top of the car.

"So now we have practice going at on the race track and we're in a car 50 feet below the race track, upside down with a bunch of the safety fence gone. We started laughing so hard we could barely function. Now, as we all know, Bill was a pretty serious guy, but remember, we were 35 years younger.

"We finally got the door open on my side...facing toward the moon...and crawled out. Meanwhile, they had put out the red flag, stopping practice. Here comes a wrecker, the ambulance, officials, everyone. And there we are, me and Bill, standing there in slacks, dress shoes, and silk shirts, which I guess were fashionable at the time. Then they all realized it was me and Bill. They didn't know what to say.

"Bill turned to me still laughing. I mean, what we did was so ridiculous. He asked, 'You know what this is?' I said, 'Well, it's a mess.' He said, 'Hell no, this is a sign of two true executives. Come on, pal. Let's go to the race track.'"

"There was a West Coast newspaper journalist who had done a lot for NASCAR over the years, Gordon Martin in San Francisco. Back in 1998, Bill Jr. was out that way for the truck series banquet. We started talking, and Bill asked about Gordon, wanted to know how he was doing because he knew he'd been sick. I told Bill that Gordon was in the hospital and in bad shape.

"Well, we had a full afternoon of meetings scheduled for that day. We had a lot of things we needed to do; it was on a Friday. Bill asked me if I thought it would mean anything to Gordon if we canceled out some of our stuff and went to go see him. I told Bill that I thought Gordon would recognize us and yes, that it probably would mean a lot to him. Bill then decided that we were going to rearrange the schedule that day so we could go see an old friend.

"It was only a couple miles to the hospital from the hotel where we were staying. Martin indeed recognized us, and I know he appreciated the visit because a bit later on, when he got a little better—call it a 5 out of 10 instead of a 2 out of 10—he brought up the visit to me. He told me it meant a lot to him.

"When we left the hospital, Bill turned to me and asked if Gordon needed anything. 'Just a break, just some better health going his way,' I said. Bill said, 'If he needs anything, you just let me know.'

"I understood Bill's message to me, what he was trying to get across. I'm sure if I'd ever called Bill to say Gordon had run out of money or insurance, he would've helped immediately.

"Bill had a real heart, let me tell you. That's the point of this story."

Geri McMullin, Bill France Jr.'s secretary, 1984–2007

"There are so, so many stories I could tell from our years together, but one of my favorites comes from not that long ago, 2003, the week of the Sprint Cup banquet in New York City in December. This was very personal for me.

"This was at a time when Bill was not at his best physically, and he asked my son, John Jr., to accompany us to New York to be there to give him a hand if he needed anything. In the process, he really took joy in showing John New York. John was in his glory for a few days, let me tell you.

"John and I flew up to New York with Bill Jr. and Betty Jane on their plane. He took us to lunch when we landed. He took us to Zabar's Market, the famous gourmet food place on the Upper West Side; he really wanted John to experience that. He took us to the famous Chinese restaurant, Mr. K's, for dinner. Stevie Wonder was there eating the night we went. Bill Jr. had John sit right next to him during dinner. Bill loved taking people out to dinner because he always ordered everything for everybody. John, who was 22 at the time, was like his father back then—a meat and potatoes guy. Well, Bill had him eating everything, Peking Duck and these other different things on the menu. Another night he took us to a great Italian restaurant, and Bill had John eating his personal favorite dish, Dover Sole—and John hates fish.

"I guess, that week, he was like a mentor to John, teaching him about New York. Now John loves going to New York and going to Mr. K's himself, taking people there and showing him Bill Jr.'s chopsticks. Yes, Bill still has his own pair of chopsticks there. You pull out this drawer, and there they are with his name on them.

"Bill Jr. took John under his wing that week. It really touched my heart. Bill taught him the good life, I suppose you could say. Now John's still living it—on his beer pocketbook."

Paul Brooks, NASCAR Senior Vice President

"Every now and then I will get asked about what college I attended. Well, I didn't attend college, so a lot of times I'll just tell people, 'I went to WCF University.'

"Sometimes they don't ask any further but when they do, I don't hesitate. I'll tell them 'WCF—William Clifton France University, the best education in the world.'

"And I mean that. I wouldn't trade the education I got from Bill Jr. for anything."

Mike Joy, former Motor Racing Network broadcaster, current FOX broadcaster

"I was honored to know Bill France Jr. as my boss when I was at MRN and much later as my friend. That makes it doubly hard to write about a man who, from my perspective, had two distinct, intertwined personalities.

"As a boss, he was tough but always fair. He would continually challenge you to do your best and to think things all the way through.

"'Make sure the trouble's worth the trouble,' Bill would often say, a not-so-gentle reminder to us that the upside of a particular endeavor should justify the effort and expense.

"He was great at analyzing a deal and cutting right to the chase. When a supplier was going to provide us some services without charge, Bill asked, 'How much does it cost if it's free?'

"We had a couple of knock-down drag-outs, one over something I wrote, and one over something I described on the air. That put me on the receiving end of Bill's famed, 'You might need this sport more than it needs you' speech. I've since found out that puts me in some pretty good company.

"In later years, I think my passion for the sport and respect for its history led us to become friends, though he never hesitated to set me straight if I strayed off course in his opinion.

"'Charlotte wasn't the first superspeedway with lights, Raleigh Fairgrounds was,' Bill chided me a few days after an All-Star race telecast. I was in grammar school when they last raced at Raleigh, but he expected me to know these things.

"We had a great conversation on the evening of the last Sprint Cup banquet he attended. As I shook his hand to leave, Bill, with Betty Jane on his arm, said, 'You've done alright. We're proud of you.'

"If he was here today, I would tell him this:

"The pleasure was all mine."

Chapter Twenty-Six

The Lion in Winter

Bill France Jr., a man who could afford to travel the world whenever he pleased, preferred to spend the majority of his time in Daytona Beach, Florida, during his last years, in a new house built next door to his old house.

Granted, whatever wanderlust remained in the old man had diminished greatly with the advances of age and illness. Nonetheless, there is a distinct air of serendipity with Bill Jr.'s late-life plight working to keep him at home by necessity instead of choice.

Home for Bill Jr. was indeed where his heart was.

"An interesting side of Bill was the love he had for Daytona Beach," said Daytona Beach mayor Glenn Ritchey. "Bill was someone who didn't ever forget where he came from. He certainly had the financial means to have lived anywhere but chose to live in the town where he grew up."

"But he didn't just *live* in Daytona Beach. He was involved and had relationships throughout the city. His involvement was in ways that were beneficial to the entire Daytona Beach community, and he never sought attention or recognition for his good works. He could have easily said he was too busy, but he never did. When he committed to a cause or activity, he was fully committed.

"Whenever our town found itself in need of help, Bill followed in the tradition of the France family to answer that need."

Some of Bill Jr.'s answers included steadfast support of the annual London Symphony Orchestra/Boston Pops music festival in Daytona Beach. That support was recognized in 2009 when a concert was performed in his honor. The following tribute was included in the program for the concert:

> William Clifton France was a man whose all-business exterior belied the heart that beat within, a heart that reserved ample room for his family, his friends—and his community.

Never one to wear his philanthropy on his sleeve, "Bill Jr." quietly supported causes that in his mind mattered most to the place he called home. The London Symphony Orchestra was one of those causes.

Bill Jr. arrived in Daytona Beach in October 1934, riding along in the family car. He was 18 months old. His father, "Big Bill" France, took up residence here and went about making history by founding NASCAR and transforming a sleepy beachside community into the World Center of Racing.

Making history, then, came to Bill Jr. more or less naturally. He followed his father as NASCAR's leader and decided to also make Daytona his home.

Along the way, Bill Jr. made his home better.

Most everyone knows how he spearheaded NASCAR's growth. Not everyone knows about how he helped grow the Daytona Beach International Festival into a nationally renowned musical event, with LSO performances complemented by local outreach and educational activities. His support of the LSO was steadfast for more than 25 years until his death in 2007 at the age of 74.

You want eclectic? Bill Jr. dropped the green flag for both stock cars and culture in this community.

You want eclectic? Bill Jr. loved the Daytona 500 AND the London Symphony Orchestra Pops.

William Clifton France is remembered—and revered—for his efforts that took a mainly Southeastern sport of stock car racing and turned it into a national phenomenon.

But tonight's program is also about remembrance—and reverence—for a remarkable man whose true legacy resides as much in the music you hear each year at the Daytona Beach International Festival, as it does in the thunder of race cars at Daytona International Speedway.

Bill France Jr. and the London Symphony Orchestra—a strange combination at first glance, right? This revelation, to some, may seem akin to the news of several years ago that Junior Johnson, the ol' moonshine runner himself, had become a collector of fine wines.

Indeed, Bill Jr. enjoyed the music in large part because he knew his daughter Lesa *loved* it. But what he really enjoyed was being a player in making the music festival a fixture in his city.

Community involvement manifested elsewhere. In the summer of 1998, raging wildfires blanketed the Daytona Beach area in smoke. It was so bad that NASCAR had to postpone its annual July 4 weekend race—slated to be held for the first time under the newly installed lights at Daytona International Speedway—until October. The city—Bill's city—was basically under siege. Power outages were frequent, and Florida Power & Light crews worked around the clock to restore electricity. Bill Jr. made sure the Speedway facilities were available for FPL to store equipment during the crisis.

He also had a hand in dispatching International Speedway Corporation food-service personnel to the Gulf Coast in 2005 after Hurricane Katrina ravaged the region to help feed police and rescue workers.

"We have a lot of capabilities to help people in need…we feel like we have a corporate obligation to help, and we take that obligation very seriously…it's all about being good corporate citizens—or good citizens, period," Bill Jr. said in 2005, speaking at a gathering of young business leaders. (Note: The speech, one of the last he gave, is reproduced in the chapter, "Speeches.")

"The City of Daytona Beach has been good to the racing business," he continued. "But there's no doubt that the racing business has been good to the city. We want to keep it that way. So, as you can imagine, we want—and need—to keep driving our business. But we also want to take this city along for the ride."

When Bill Jr. officially stepped down from the Chairman/CEO position in October 2003, handing over the leadership role to his son Brian, there also was a switching of offices between the two men. It was somewhat symbolic, but there was also a practicality to the trade-off, as the chairman's work space was adjacent to those of NASCAR vice chairman Jim France, NASCAR president Mike Helton, and NASCAR chief operating officer George Pyne.

But from the outset of the switch, it was well-known that while Bill Jr. had moved down the hall, he had by no means gone out the door. A couple of different perceptions developed within the industry—and mainly with the media—regarding just what was going on over at International Speedway Boulevard behind closed doors. Extremes—that's what those perceptions were. Depending on who you talked to, Bill Jr. had either completely removed himself from the day-to-day operations of NASCAR or was still actively involved in the company's decision-making process.

Brian France describes things as being "in the middle" of those two extremes after he took over and before his father's health worsened. "You had the normal give and take between two people in that sort of situation," Brian said. After all, he'd run the business for 30 years, and even though I was coming in, he still had a lot of input to share.

"But at the same time, he realized I needed some autonomy. Still, something like that is going to be an awkward time if you're trying to do things right— which he was. He still had tendencies to want to go back to the way things used to be and was pretty explicit that something needed to be done this way or that way. I mean, he'd been involved in the sport his whole life.

"We got a lot done together, even though we may have differed on how to get things done. Probably every major decision I had to make, I would check in with him in some way, not necessarily for his complete approval but at least for his point of view, even if I knew he was going to have a different point of view than I did. Certainly if I was ever in trouble with something or had a big problem, he would be the first call I'd make. Yeah...I relied on him a lot."

That reliance notwithstanding, the business of running NASCAR continued with Bill France Jr. increasingly on the periphery, partly because of his wavering health, partly because there was simply so much going on in so many directions.

The old ruler kept bouncing back. And whenever his health improved, so did his demeanor. In January 2003, many people got a glimpse of the Bill Jr. of old at NASCAR's now-annual preseason event during the Charlotte Media Tour at the NASCAR Research and Development Center in Concord, North Carolina. Unfortunately, it came at the expense of his son, in the opinion of many at the event that day.

Brian France was then NASCAR's executive vice president, riding atop a wave of success, with George Pyne, Mike Helton, and Paul Brooks as his main sidekicks. At the time, NASCAR was starting the third year of the epic network television contract with FOX, TNT, and NBC. Ratings were on the rise, as was attendance. Work on safety initiatives was constant; the year before during the media tour, the R&D Center was officially unveiled. Head and neck restraints were mandated. Work was proceeding on the installation of the SAFER barrier systems (commonly called soft walls) at all tracks hosting NASCAR national series races. Sponsorship was booming. Basically, Brian Zachary France was feeling his oats, which he had every right to.

But on that day, so was his father.

Brian was amid a presentation that was being called unofficially a "state of the sport" rundown. Everything was progressing normally in front of 250 or so members of the media. That contingent included representatives from many outlets that, years before, would have never considered covering such an event. This was a big-time audience, far removed from the old days when 50 reporters packed into a smoke-filled Kahn press room at Daytona International Speedway was considered a major deal.

Suddenly, with Brian in mid-sentence, Bill Jr. arose from his front-row seat just to the right of the center-stage podium where Brian stood. Bill Jr. turned to his right and motioned for a NASCAR public relations manager, who was one of the designated microphone "carriers." The mike was quickly brought to him as the packed room fell silent, uniformly uncertain of what they were going to hear but at the same time certain it would be interesting.

"Brian, let me help you out," Bill Jr. began, after being handed the microphone. What followed was a mini-lecture on a concept called "Realignment 2004 and Beyond" whereby the chairman—who was, incidentally, reminding people he was *still* the chairman—laid out a plan that was a tad vague but also decidedly pointed, an across-the-board warning to all race tracks involved in the NASCAR Sprint Cup Series that race dates were subject to change. But Bill Jr. also put the onus on various track ownership groups lest people got the notion that NASCAR would take an autocratic approach to adjusting the schedule.

"We are not going to take International Speedway Corporation races and give them to Speedway Motorsports Incorporated tracks, or vice versa," he said.

Bill Jr., however, made it clear that individual ownership groups could petition NASCAR for date changes if all changes involved tracks in their particular arena of control. He also let it be known that no track was immune for possible loss of a date, be it a facility owned by International Speedway Corporation, Speedway Motorsports Incorporated, or one of the smaller ownership groups.

"What we're saying is if an event is not doing as well as it could, and SMI wanted to take it somewhere else, we would entertain that," Bill Jr. said that day. "We would do this in concert with the track promoters. If they don't want to do it, they wouldn't have to. But this is a good opportunity to take an asset that is underperforming and take it somewhere else within the company. The shareholders are going to get the enhancement of that.

"One of the advantages I've had the last six months, lying in the hospital bed or at the house, is I'm watching a lot of television. And I don't like to see a lot of empty seats. If we've got a CEO or vice president of marketing considering sponsoring a car 'because this is the hottest sport going,' and then I turn on the TV and don't see anybody there or see a weak crowd, I've got to ask myself, 'What's so hot about this?'"

Bill Jr. spent five minutes or so talking on the microphone and then, in the breakout interviews that followed the formal press conference, he held court for another 45 minutes.

Later, Brian France would say he and his father had words about the interruption of the event. Brian told his father of his disappointment and his embarrassment in front of the motorsports media, who of course reported the impromptu speech by the chairman in-depth.

Bill France Jr. had flexed his muscles for one of the last times, and it would not be forgotten anytime soon.

In July 2003, Bill Jr. was in his final two months as NASCAR's chairman and CEO—a position he assumed in 2000 when the NASCAR board of directors was created and he handed off the NASCAR presidency to Mike Helton. In October 2003, he became vice chairman, giving way as his son Brian became NASCAR's third-generation leader.

Bill had one more major job to complete before stepping aside—the announcement of the company that would replace Winston as the title sponsor of NASCAR's premier series. That company was Nextel Communications. The deal was handled largely by others, starting with Brian, with Bill providing the stamp of approval. And this was basically a rubber stamp because, despite his long-time allegiance to R.J. Reynolds, Bill Jr. recognized the need for a change to facilitate marketing initiatives and boost overall appeal of NASCAR. Nextel and all its possibilities fit on a personal level as well for the aging boss. He had become a bit of a senior citizen "techie" and was enamored with the Internet, computers, Palm Pilots, and cell phones. And he wasn't just enamored; he was competent and thorough when it came to taking advantage of what technology could offer him. With apologies to Nextel, he had a cell phone account with every major carrier to make sure that, wherever he traveled, he would always have coverage.

The Nextel deal was mammoth, a 10-year contract worth millions to NASCAR. It was announced on June 19, 2003, in a big-time setting—New York City—with none other than Bill France Jr. holding court.

"Nextel is a perfect fit for NASCAR because technology is an untapped area within our sport," Bill Jr. told the crowd of media packed into NASDAQ's Manhattan headquarters.

"There's going to be a lot of positive things come out of this," Bill Jr. said later in an interview with NASCAR.com's Marty Smith. "This is rewarding, to see this happen. We're just optimistic about everything [with this deal]."

While Bill Jr. provided the punctuation, his son Brian had handled the negotiation. "Bill Jr. created an environment for Brian and others to succeed in areas like this," said NASCAR senior vice president Paul Brooks.

And, just as he did with the chief players at R.J. Reynolds, Bill Jr. struck up fast friendships with his new associates at Nextel, particularly the company's CEO at the time, Tim Donahue.

Donahue seemed a bit like a modern-day Ralph Seagraves, perhaps explaining why he and Bill Jr. hit it off so well. Gregarious to a fault, Donahue, like Bill Jr., loved to tell stories and socialize. He enjoyed a cocktail or two and also enjoyed making friends, starting with the chairman of NASCAR.

"Nextel catered to small and mid-sized businesses around the country, and NASCAR had huge appeal to our customers," Donahue said. "We had explored various opportunities to enter the sport, including a car sponsorship, but for various reasons we passed on those opportunities. When the series sponsorship became available, we jumped at it.

"Bill Jr. and a number of NASCAR officials joined me and my team for a dinner in Washington to discuss a potential partnership. Bill began the conversation talking about the history of NASCAR, and I was struck by his infectious passion for the sport. His love for NASCAR and his commitment to the sport were evident as he walked us through his vision of this great American phenomenon and what it could do for our company. It was one of the most memorable and enjoyable business dinners I've ever attended.

"What I admired most about Bill was his straightforward, no-nonsense approach to the subject matter. Bill never danced around a topic. He clearly articulated his position but always left room for compromise if it enhanced either the fan experience or the business relationship. He was as fair minded as any business executive I have dealt with. His word was his bond, and his handshake was all that was necessary. He and Betty Jane went out of their way to make my wife Jayne, me, and the entire Nextel organization feel as if we were part of the NASCAR family. I learned a lot from Bill France. I laughed out loud at his stories. I marveled at his unique perspectives on any of life's subjects."

In the last four years of his life, from 2003–07, Bill France Jr. found a new project that fit his community activist role. The project came in the form of a 5'2", incredibly feisty woman also living out her last years on this Earth while working on a legacy of her own. Yvonne Scarlett-Golden, an African-American and Daytona Beach native, had returned to her hometown after outliving her husband and two daughters and becoming a renowned educator and civil rights activist in San Francisco, California. After returning to her hometown, she successfully ran for a seat on the Daytona Beach City Commission in 1995. In 2003, she decided she wanted to be a 77-year-old mayor, the first African-American mayor in the city, ever.

She faced challenges, to say the least.

She soon found an ally in Bill France Jr.

Let's call it what it was—an alliance based on reciprocity. The candidate knew that Bill France Jr. could deliver funding and, of course, votes. His endorsement would carry considerable weight come election time. Likewise, Bill Jr. knew the candidate could deliver support for the business community.

Soon, the alliance took a personal turn. The candidate and Bill Jr. developed a faux adversarial banter in their meetings. Two old-timers they were, taking delight in the fact that they were allies despite the fact that they were complete opposites in every way but united in their desire to help each other—and the City of Daytona Beach in the process.

Originally, Bill Jr. had declined to support Scarlett-Golden.

"He told her that she had done a good job as a city commissioner but that he didn't think the city was ready to elect a black mayor, let alone a black female mayor," said Donna Sue Sanders, Scarlett-Golden's campaign manager. "He said he wouldn't support her because he didn't want to put her in a position where she could get hurt.

"That day, she thanked Mr. France for his time, but she came back three weeks later. She told him, 'I thought a lot about [what] you told me awhile back, and I'm here to tell you that I'm running with or without your support.' Mr. France leaned back in his chair and looked at her, and suddenly a big smile came across his face. 'Well Yvonne,' he said, 'it sounds like you've made up your mind. And you know, if you're really going to do this, then you're going to need my help. So we'll do it together.'

"She was so much like him. That's why they got along so well. When she made up her mind to do something, nobody was going to sway her. I think that's what he admired about her...her tenacity, her bulldog approach."

Betty Jane France said Bill Jr. "thought Yvonne, being an African-American woman, could reconcile a lot of the racial problems going on in the community at the time. She didn't mind rolling up her sleeves and walking right into tough situations."

Scarlett-Golden won the 2003 election in a close battle, defeating Mike Shallow. Two factors brought it home—a strong African-American voter turnout and support from the Daytona Beach business community that had Bill France Jr. on the pole.

She then won reelection in 2005 in an even-closer race, edging Shallow again. Not long afterward, she was diagnosed with cancer, whereupon a brief, brave fight of another type ensued. She died December 5, 2006.

On the night of December 1, the mayor had visitors. When Bill France Jr.'s private plane touched down in Daytona Beach, having returned its party from the annual NASCAR Sprint Cup Awards Ceremony in New York, at the famed Waldorf Astoria hotel, Bill Jr. announced a little stopover before everybody headed home.

"We got off the plane, there were seven of us," Betty Jane France said. "Bill and I, the current mayor of Daytona Beach Glenn Ritchey, Hyatt Brown and his wife Connie, and Tom Staed and his wife Barbara. Bill told us we were all going by Yvonne's house. The rest of us didn't really think we should do that because she was pretty sick. But, we did.

"When we got there, she rose to the occasion. She sat right up in her bed, which I don't think she had done all day—and right away told Tom Staed that he owed her $100, which he did for something. She gave each of us a little talking to. We were amazed. And that was the last time we saw her alive."

The mayor's funeral was held on December 13 in the Mary McLeod Bethune Performing Arts Center on the campus of her alma mater Bethune-Cookman University in the heart of Daytona Beach with several thousand in attendance.

Bill France Jr. spoke at the funeral from his seat near the front of the auditorium. Clearly declining, he wasn't able to make the trek down the aisle and up the steps to the podium. Instead, a podium and microphone was set up at his seat.

Midway through the uplifting "celebration of life" service, Bill Jr. rose slowly from that seat, his wife Betty Jane assisting him. He slipped the oxygen tube away from his nose, over his head, and braced himself against the podium, leaning tentatively into the microphone. As he spoke, he struggled to catch his breath, coughing frequently. Some of his words were almost inaudible. It was shocking for some in the audience to see Bill Jr. in such decline, publicly.

Yvonne was a friend to Daytona Beach. And yes, she was a friend to business development in this city. But I'm here because she was a friend on a personal level.

She came to see me for the first time some years back when she was running for the city commission, seeking my support. She had moved back to her hometown of Daytona Beach from San Francisco, and I really didn't know much about her. So I ended up supporting the guy she was running against. Well, that guy lost.

A few years later she came back to see me again, this time because she was running for mayor. I wasn't sure this city was ready to elect an African-American mayor, and I told her that. She disagreed. She thought the city was ready to make some history and…in her unique style…told me so.

She delivered—on all fronts, proving she was a mayor of all people in this city. I've been a member of the business community here for 50 years, and the business community is proud that we supported Yvonne.

When she ran for reelection last year, she was confident again. That confidence tended to rub off on you. Even our local newspaper, the *Daytona Beach News-Journal*, realizing they had sinned the first time around by supporting her opponent, backed her reelection campaign, which was successful.

Yvonne was enthusiastic. At times, she was cantankerous. Some people might say she and I had that quality in common. And at the end of the day, she let you know she was the mayor. She used to remind me of that sometimes, when we might be at odds about something. I think she really enjoyed reminding me of that.

She was proud to be mayor. That was obvious by the way she ran her meetings and by the way she spoke with authority to 200,000 people at the Speedway right before the Daytona 500.

She was a good mayor.

More importantly, she was a good woman.

And like a lot of people, I'm going to miss her.

Thank you.

Bill Jr. slumped into his seat. He did not look well, and for those close to him and his medical situation, it was impossible not to think that his own end was fast approaching. The five minutes or so without the oxygen had taken a lot out of him.

The highlight of the service was the rousing eulogy delivered by Reverend Claude Ingram, the senior pastor at Mount Bethel Baptist Institutional Church. It was classic call-and-response, Southern Baptist style.

Said Ingram, regarding the mayor: "A mighty oak has fallen, leaving the glaring space against the sky where she stood."

In that auditorium, another oak was falling right before the eyes of everyone in attendance.

This would be Bill France Jr.'s last speaking appearance.

Things went somewhat quickly downhill from that day. While there were no more speeches, Bill Jr. would make two more ventures into public.

On February 8, riding in the motorized wheelchair that by then was a must for him to get around, Bill Jr. rolled into the spacious Daytona 500 Club tent at Daytona International Speedway adjacent to the front grandstand for NASCAR's annual Media Day. The event was first started in 2000 in response to the mushrooming popularity of the sport that would be boosted even further in 2001, the first year of the epic network television contract Bill Jr. helped broker. Several hundred media members, including an increasing international contingent, work the event that is patterned in part after the much-more frenzied Super Bowl Media Day. It's important to note that the NFL allows members of the NASCAR Communications Department to attend their event to pick up on ideas or procedures that might be helpful. The NFL and NASCAR in a working relationship—somewhere Big Bill France must be smiling at that. Bill Jr. did.

At NASCAR Media Day, all of NASCAR's top drivers attend and are scheduled into individual interview sessions with newspapers, magazines, television. and radio. It's an all-day affair and has become absolutely vital to kicking off each NASCAR season, starting with the season-opening Daytona 500.

A mid-day appearance at Media Day by Bill Jr. became a tradition, with him generally remaining in the lunch area as reporters crowded around, jostling for precious position, jamming microphones and recorders in his direction, eager to ask questions and knowing they would get lively, forthright answers.

This final Media Day interview session was different. Bill, riding on his bright red motorized scooter, was brought in by friend Earl Tisdale and NASCAR vice president Jim Hunter. The sight of the oxygen tank and breathing tube, as it had been at the mayor's funeral, was disconcerting to some. Several media members admitted later that they avoided joining the session because of the way Bill looked. Said one writer, who had known Bill Jr. for years and seldom missed a chance to interview him, "I just didn't want to bother him."

Only four writers came over to the table—Nate Ryan of *USA Today*, David Newton of ESPN.com, Brant James of the *St. Petersburg Times*, and Ken Willis of the *Daytona Beach News-Journal*. Hunter, laughing at it now, recalled, "Bill was really pissed off that so few people came over to talk to him." That reaction was of course vintage Bill France Jr., who knew he was likely making his last visit to an event that personified his vision for the growth of NASCAR.

"I got the sense that he wanted to talk to us and wanted to give us his opinion, but he was really laboring at that point," Ryan said. "He had his breathing apparatus on, with the oxygen. He would pause maybe after every eight or 10 words. He would take deep breaths after every answer. When you go back and listen to the recording of the interview, it's hard to make out what he's saying. The other half-dozen times I was in an interview situation with Bill, let's just say it wasn't nearly as hard to understand what he was saying. But he seemed sharp still. He was asking David Newton about traffic numbers for ESPN.com."

Which was also vintage Bill Jr. stuff, turning an interview session into a give-and-take. While he was computer and Internet-savvy, he was still coming to grips with certain aspects of "new media." Dot-com media coverage was the ultimate unknown quantity for a man who years before had pasted flyers onto telephone poles to drive attendance by both newspaper reporters and fans.

"How many readers you got reading that thing [ESPN.com] every day?" Bill Jr. asked Newton, who replied, "Six million hits a day."

Bill Jr., ever the skeptic, came back with, "So, that's three million people in and out, right?"

Here's what the *Times'* James wrote about that exchange, "France was seemingly satisfied—but not necessarily impressed."

The session was relatively brief, only 15 minutes or so, and the conversation was disjointed due to Bill Jr.'s limitations. But there were some takeaways for the writers. Bill Jr. joked about veteran driver James Hylton being only a year younger than him and still racing, and that maybe he needed to get on Hylton's training program.

Looking back, the fact that it was a special half-hour is not lost on Ryan. "That was the last time we had him on record, commenting about NASCAR," Ryan said, adding his own personal takeaway from the day.

"I think he went out of his way to make an especially important point. Here's how he put it to us: 'I'm glad I stepped away when I did and put Brian in charge. He's doing a good job. I'm glad I'm out of the picture now because I'd have a hard time keeping up, I'm just sucking air now.'"

Added Ryan, "I felt like he understood his time was near. He seemed at peace, that he had passed the torch at the right time."

February 12, a Monday evening at the Daytona Club inside Daytona International Speedway, marked Bill France Jr.'s final public appearance. The event was aptly titled; "Roast & Toast Bill France Hot Dog Dinner," honoring Bill Jr.'s lifelong affinity for the great American delicacy. The event benefited the NASCAR Foundation, NASCAR's charitable arm which is chaired by Betty Jane France. A variety of businesses and individuals paid $7,500 per table. They likely would've paid thousands more.

Many of Bill Jr.'s closest friends, along with his immediate family members, attended. They all had to know that time was growing short for the man they so admired. Attendees listened to a string of amusing and personal stories.

For many, it was the last time they would see Bill Jr.

Chapter Twenty-Seven

Safe at Home

Geri McMullin remembers the bright spring day as one of the darkest in NASCAR history, as far as she knows it.

"March 13, 2007...that was his last day in the office," she said.

McMullin isn't likely to forget the date. "It was my birthday...Bill was at home and called the office. He asked me what I wanted for my birthday. I told him I wanted him to come into the office and he did. He forced himself to come in. I felt really bad afterward because he did. But he made the effort. His nurse, along with his good friend Earl Tisdale, brought him in. He only stayed for a couple of hours. I didn't realize how badly he was feeling at the time.

"After that day, he didn't come back again."

Bill Jr. had gathered himself and made the short but arduous trip to his office to fulfill McMullin's request. But maybe he was looking for an excuse to come in one more time, to sit in that chair at the head of that table, and remember the days when his every word was law in the hell-bent world of stock car racing. McMullin should perhaps feel no guilt for requesting his presence that day. She might well have been doing him a favor, providing the emotional nudge needed for him to make one final trip.

At that point, Bill France Jr. had less than three months to live. He spent that time in his home on the Halifax River—their "dream home" as Betty Jane France wistfully calls it.

"Bill loved this house and he loved being here, just staying at home," she said.

Bill Jr.'s final four months were marked in NASCAR's Daytona Beach offices by an emptiness that pervaded the hallways. To gauge his status day-to-day, one only had to walk down to his office, which was silent but still retained its sentry in McMullin. On any given day, the look on her face could provide the latest update with no words needed.

176

The sense of dread permeated the place. Even the ever-optimistic PR man Jim Hunter was out of spin material. "I think Bill's given up…I think he's just tired of being so sick," Hunter said one afternoon, at a time of day that would've been primetime for one of Bill Jr.'s impromptu visits. In recent years, Hunter had missed a number of those visits, whereupon Bill Jr. would invariably half-yell an inquiry about Hunter's whereabouts loud enough for a couple of hallways to hear, with a gratuitous profanity tossed in for good measure. His query usually included a dig, suggesting that Hunter was probably "out on the damn golf course again." Often, Bill Jr. was right about that.

Bill France Jr. had gone home where he would get the care he needed right to the end—home to 1600 Peninsula Drive. When someone from the house calls a NASCAR or ISC extension, the caller ID function reads, "1600 Penn," just like that other big-time residence in Washington, D.C. The ID was Bill Jr.'s idea as a joke—but also as a way to make sure employees would notice when a call came from him or Betty Jane.

He had gone home where he and his wife would entertain only a handful of times during those last months. "Toward the end," Betty Jane remembered, "everybody wanted to come and visit, but I just had to put a stop to it eventually. We just couldn't do it anymore after a while."

Lesa Kennedy stopped by to see her father on the morning of May 24, 2007—her birthday.

"It was the last time I saw him when you could say he was coherent," she said. "I went by to talk with him for a little bit, and he invited me to stay on for lunch that day. I wasn't able to do that, but I told him I'd be right back.

"Then, when I came back, he wasn't unconscious but he wasn't really with the program. He had gone downhill quickly. I was only gone for about an hour.

"That day was the last time I talked to him."

Lesa seems comforted by the fact that her father was able to die at home. She points out that in his last few years, his world had shrunk.

"As his illness developed, he started being focused more locally," she said. "He didn't travel as much. He became more sentimental about the Daytona Beach area."

Brian France knew his father's life was nearing an end after a visit two weeks before his death. Two years later, the son's memory is vivid, and it is one tempered by sadness but strengthened in a strange way by the knowledge that he had witnessed something revealing not only about his father's life but human existence in general. Brian France was allowed to peer through a window at whatever faced his gravely ill father on the other side.

Here's Brian's emotional retelling of the experience:

"He'd been upstairs at his house and, at the time, it had become difficult for him to come downstairs for a glass of water or to sit out on the patio area, which when I came over we would normally do, he, Mom, and I.

"When I came over, there would typically be an issue of the day to discuss, and normally he would have a lot of opinions and a lot of things to say.

"Not this time."

Brian recalls his father coming downstairs, perfectly groomed and dressed all in black, Johnny Cash–like almost. Sunglasses, too, even though it was around 6:00 PM.

"He didn't look that bad," Brian said. "But you could tell he was, well, *leaving*. Clearly, he had gone. He wasn't there. He was just staring into the moonlight. He was not himself.

"Later on that night, when I thought about it, I realized that he was in the ninth inning at that point as far as his *being* went. I had never seen that sort of thing before. People who have had loved ones and seen the last few percent of their life go by in front of them know what I mean by that.

"It was a sad thing. Normally I would've given him information, and even in tough moments he still would've had a quick opinion. But this time he just stared at me, nodding, saying, 'Uh-huh, uh-huh, uh-huh.'

"He was one step away from being with the angels. Thing is, he looked fine, but it was like there was no one in his body. It was very strange."

Did Bill Jr. know the end was closing in? If he did, he wasn't about to let on.

"He was the kind of guy who wasn't going to get really mushy or deep with you," Brian said. "He had this lane he was in [and] he wasn't going to change that. Here's the deal—you knew he loved everybody, but he was still John Wayne, by God, all the way until the end. I think he looked at death like he looked at life, very pragmatically. It was like everybody had a time limit and you needed to do your life's work and what matters with your family and one day, one day if you're lucky, the end of it comes late in life. If not, that's the way it goes. There wasn't a lot of sentiment or reflections with my dad."

Brian France seems to wish there had been.

"Maybe his attitude about death cushioned the blow for *him*. But for his family, I think we would've liked to hear more reflections. As opposed to him saying things like, 'The calendar is about to get me' maybe we could've heard more things like how much he loved our mother."

Paul Brooks can't bring himself to erase the voice mail on his cell phone. It's from the morning of June 4, 2007. It was left by a tearful Davis Hamilton, the France's personal assistant, who helps run the household at 1600 Peninsula.

"Paul, this is Davis…it's happened. Call me at the house."

Bill France Jr. was dead at the age of 74.

The death was announced during the running of the NASCAR Sprint Cup Series race at Dover (Delaware) International Speedway, which had been postponed from the day before. And how just was that, to have the announcement concurrent with cars racing around the track in one of the country's bigger markets?

The tributes from the media were overwhelming. The requisite criticism, or at the very least the skepticism that had marked much of the media coverage during Bill Jr.'s time, was virtually non-existent. With the great old man finally gone, the press had little choice but to reflect on the big picture. And to their everlasting credit, they did just that.

"Bill Jr. knew where he wanted the sport to go and how he wanted it to get there," wrote the *Tampa (Florida) Tribune's* award-winning columnist, Martin Fennelly. "He put NASCAR all over TV, all over the country, into cities everywhere."

That was one reaction. Here are a few others:

> "France mostly came across as interesting and interested and unpretentious as a worn tire…. He was used to getting his way. But he didn't act high and mighty. He could be a steamroller. But he was a good listener, too…. For a dictator, he was a pretty good guy.

"Not until France died did he cease moving forward. That was his spirit and business model—and his nuts-and-bolts genius. He's the pragmatist who steered stock car racing from Main Street to Wall Street. He's the maestro who orchestrated a sport's transformation from regional fascination to national brand.

"His father was Big Bill, the larger-than-life creator of NASCAR. But Bill Jr. was the true giant."

—Bob Lipper, *Richmond Times-Dispatch*

"While Bill France Jr. built NASCAR into a huge business and the country's biggest spectator sport, he built it into something else, too. Something perhaps even more important.... As NASCAR roars round the track, it climbs ever higher in the public's affection and esteem. It celebrates things about the American character—power, speed, courage, risk-taking, fun—that we are reluctant to surrender, at least psychically. And thanks to Bill France Jr., it celebrates national inclusiveness.

"Many of us didn't know what we were missing—until he showed it to us."

—Robert Sullivan, *Time* magazine

"Bill France Jr. could intimidate with a look or a gesture. And when running the show his father founded, no relationship got in the way of doing business.... The man was just as comfortable eating a hot dog in an old gas station or signing autographs on pit row as he was lobbying sponsors on Madison Avenue or dressing down a driver in the garage."

—Michael Smith, Street & Smith's *Sports Business Journal*

"In his prime, Bill France Jr.—in Southern-speak 'Billy Jr.'—was a formidable presence. But he kept the common touch with drivers, car owners, and reporters. His informal Sunday morning pre-race bull sessions with the media at the NASCAR hauler are still talked about. So is his ability to make a decision that might have seemed to fly in the face of logic but that upon reflection made common sense."

—Mike Mulhern, *Winston-Salem Journal*

"Bill France Jr. has been portrayed as a visionary, but his great secret was that he was not. He was a common man who saw through the eyes of the common man, thought with the uncluttered mind of the common man, empathized entirely with what excited the common man. It was all about the show."

—Ed Hinton, *Chicago Tribune*

"He was a leader with unlimited power who wielded it for the universal good. The good of NASCAR was always paramount in his mind. No team, no driver—not Richard Petty, not Dale Earnhardt—was bigger than NASCAR. Nor was France. Nor did he want to be."

—Bill Center, *San Diego Union-Tribune*

"How many people have two ultra-successful careers during their lifetime? Bill France Jr. took two family businesses and turned them into a multi-billion dollar industry. With a company in each hand (NASCAR and ISC), he took both to new heights."

—Godwin Kelly, *Daytona Beach News-Journal*

"To take work away from Bill France Jr. would be like taking beer away from a bar hound. He was happiest when he was in the middle of whatever was going on, whether it was in the tower running a race, in his office cajoling sponsors, in the NASCAR trailer correcting drivers, or in the speedway office planning the next phase of growth."

—Mike Hembree, *NASCAR Scene*

A response emerged even from the nation's capitol. President George W. Bush had been annually welcoming the new NASCAR Sprint Cup Series champion to the White House by then, and the president and his staff had a solid awareness of the sport's popularity. The White House issued this statement:

"Laura and I are deeply saddened by the death of Bill France Jr. Bill was a legend in the world of NASCAR whose passion and vision for stock car racing led the sport to the national prominence it enjoys today

"Bill brought racing's excitement to millions of new fans through his steadfast and innovative leadership. Bill also helped ensure that the NASCAR

181

community found many ways to support the men and women of the U.S. Armed Forces. Our thoughts and prayers are with the France family."

When Bill Jr. died, a plan already in place was put into action. Brooks guided an all-out effort, involving both NASCAR and the International Speedway Corporation, to organize Bill Jr.'s funeral, which was held on June 7, only three days after his passing.

"The funeral was a testament to Bill," Brooks said. "It was representative of what he used to say about the races: the show must go on. At that point, we had a mission to complete. We put in motion the sort of process Bill had taught us: map things out, fight through whatever personal emotions, do your job. We had to make it all come together, and we did so with the leadership of Mike Helton and the whole team. We had to put something together with the right focus, the right dignity.

"One thing was certain: We were going to get it right."

Mission accomplished.

"It was perfect, just perfect," Betty Jane France said, when asked about Bill Jr.'s funeral service that was held in the same facility that had hosted mayor Yvonne Scarlett-Golden's funeral seven months prior.

It lasted about an hour. Bill Jr. would've considered that okay. Maybe. As Daytona Beach mayor Glenn Ritchey reminded the crowd of a couple thousand, Bill was always worried about "burning daylight," his slang for wasting time when there was work that could be done.

Bethune-Cookman University's concert chorale started the service with a moving piece. In addition to Ritchey, Betty Jane France and Rick Hendrick spoke, staying above the emotional fray as Bill Jr. would've liked it. Singer Edwin McCain performed "I'll Be." And as the service closed, a soprano soloist's simple but inevitably moving rendition of "Amazing Grace" was the backdrop for the exit of Betty Jane, Brian, Lesa, and the rest of the family. Pallbearers included Mike Helton, Felix Sabates, and Daytona Beach businessmen Tom Staed and Hyatt Brown.

Hendrick recounted the story of the Bodine-Earnhardt meeting re-created in *Days of Thunder*. And during his brief talk, he touched on all the aspects that made up the remarkable life of Bill Jr. Hendrick called him a mentor, a leader, a friend, a bear—and a teddy bear.

Hendrick spoke to a crowd that included Richard Petty, Darrell Waltrip, Ned Jarrett, Bobby and Donnie Allison, Dale Earnhardt Jr., Jimmie Johnson, Dale Jarrett, Michael Waltrip, Kurt Busch, Jeff Gordon, Carl Edwards, and Bill Elliott.

Bill Jr. was laid to rest in a mausoleum at a cemetery in Daytona Beach, Florida. The mausoleum was built before his death, with Paul Brooks shepherding the project home—and shielding the family from much of the emotional turmoil that would result from such a task.

"It's beautiful," Betty Jane said. "It was hard to get through, building it while Bill was still alive. The only thing that got me through it was knowing that I'd be in there too one day."

∽

Lizzy misses Bill Jr.

The Cavalier King Charles Spaniel was Bill France Jr.'s dog and the chosen one of the three King Charles Spaniels that found their way into the home and the hearts of the couple in those last years. After Bill Jr. died, Lizzy wasn't the same for a long time. She still isn't really, according to Betty Jane. Like so many humans, she wished Bill Jr. would walk through the door again.

Lizzy is only seven years old. But she has a muzzle full of gray, which appeared in the months after Bill Jr. died. Betty Jane has talked to the vets and the consensus is that the dog's instincts, after her master went away for good, may have caused her to fret- -and her hair to go gray far too prematurely. The animal knew nothing of a man who ruled a major sport with an iron fist, whose language made the sea seem like fresh water. She knew only a kindly, aging gentleman who treated her with love.

Bill France Jr. and his dogs? He bought one, then another, then another yet, all under the auspices that they were for Betty Jane.

His wife knew better.

She saw the mellowing of "her Bill" in those final years. She knew that despite the fuss he put up about caring for the dogs, he loved every minute of it, right down to giving the okay for adding a small room for the dogs—an indoor doghouse of sorts.

These days, the evenings at 1600 Peninsula are mostly quiet. Day's end is a time for Betty Jane to especially enjoy the animals. They patrol the patio that overlooks the Halifax River as the sunset in the West bathes Daytona Beach in a

183

surreal yellow-orange glow. Betty Jane feeds them treats. You wonder if Lizzy still waits for Bill Jr. to come walking in through the front door.

What a strange, surprising way to get a firm grasp on the ultimate finality of a man's death...in the graying face of a dog, whose sad eyes say more than words ever could.

Betty Jane France looks out across the Atlantic, riding the waves in *Hibanx*, the boat she and Bill Jr. bought in the 1990s. She completely remodeled the craft several years ago, rather than buy something newer and bigger. "Why get a new boat? That's what I told Bill. We liked this one."

It was the boat where Bill France Jr. held court so many times for so many years, entertaining giants of the NASCAR industry, people named Earnhardt and Hendrick and Gordon and Wallace and Sabates and, of course, France... creating an atmosphere that was decidedly un-giant-like. The fishing trips were business and fun and camaraderie all combined into something so special that the people who were once invited now speak in almost reverent tones about the excursions—even though the times they had were largely full of irreverence.

The trips are fewer now, the guest list is smaller, and not much fishing is done anymore. The nights are quieter than they ever were when Bill Jr. was alive. That often leaves Betty Jane alone on the water with her thoughts...and her memories.

On this night, the late-autumn Atlantic breeze is blowing. The holidays are only weeks away. Betty Jane will soon be spending her second Christmas without her husband of 50 years.

"The first year we were married, in 1957, I got up on Christmas morning, and there in the driveway was a '58 Chevrolet Impala," she said. "Black...white leather interior. It was beautiful. I'll never forget that car. What a surprise on our first Christmas together.

"As the years went on, Bill would ask me what I wanted for Christmas every year, and a lot of times I didn't know what to say because I didn't feel like I needed anything more than I already had. So some years on Christmas, there wouldn't be any presents from Bill. Instead, there would be a letter. Each year he would write a letter to me at Christmas.

"Those letters…," Betty Jane continued, tears rolling down her cheeks meeting a smile that made her look like it was 1957 all over again. "Those letters…they were always so personal and so important to me. He said things in those letters he never would say face to face.

"I don't have that car anymore, but you better believe that I still have every one of those letters…*every* one."

Postscript

By H.A. Branham

One must wonder what Bill France Jr. would have had to say when the inaugural class of inductees for the NASCAR Hall of Fame was announced on October 14, 2009.

After hours of deliberation in downtown Charlotte, North Carolina, by a voting panel representing constituencies from throughout the NASCAR industry—including the media—ballots were tabulated by the noted accounting firm Ernst and Young. That firm was on hand not because of the intense math involved but rather to demonstrate the complete legitimacy of the voting process.

Immediately, there was controversy—and Bill France Jr. was in the center of it, albeit posthumously.

Five inductees were announced

Richard Petty and Dale Earnhardt were in—no argument there over the two seven-time NASCAR Sprint Cup Series champions. They were on *everyone's* unofficial ballot.

The legendary driver/owner Junior Johnson, the one-time moonshiner who actually did some jail time for his involvement in that endeavor, made it, too. While not considered a certainty going into the voting, tabbing Johnson was also cool. The former outlaw, who came to personify an outlaw sport perhaps more than anyone, was now receiving the ultimate stamp of legitimacy that he said was better even than the presidential pardon he received for his moonshining conviction.

Bill France Sr.'s selection—another slam-dunk. No way could NASCAR's founder and first president be kept out of the first class. That would be Hall of Fame heresy, indeed.

Your fifth and final inductee: William Clifton France.

And the debate began.

Bill Jr. had nudged out people like David Pearson, Cale Yarborough, Bobby Allison, and Darrell Waltrip.

It was a surprise. Most people following the process probably expected Bill Jr. to be inducted the second time around in lieu of competitors like Pearson or Yarborough.

Richard Petty, by the way, inadvertently fueled the fire of debate after the announcements, disagreeing vehemently with the exclusion of his old rival, Pearson.

Media members who were involved in the voting process later described that during the pre-vote discussions, support for Bill Jr. built as the day wore on and that his proponents on the voting panel made sure to remind everyone of his accomplishments.

As if anyone needed to be reminded.

What would Bill Jr. say about this? He likely would say little publicly, while privately he would have to be proud to be entering the Hall alongside his father.

The official induction ceremony is set for May 2010, coinciding with the opening of the NASCAR Hall of Fame in Charlotte, whereupon the debate will no doubt begin anew.

On the other hand, there is little doubt what Bill would say about another announcement that came on the same day as the Hall of Fame results: *Forbes* magazine named Bill Jr.'s daughter, ISC's CEO Lesa France Kennedy, the Most Powerful Woman in Sports.

He would've been filled with pride that the little girl who grew up to work alongside and learn the business from her grandmother, Annie B., had been so honored.

And as far as *this* announcement was concerned, Bill Jr. would've had no patience for debate whatsoever.

October 14, 2009.

What a day.

Epilogue

By Jim France

Bill France Jr. was a lot of things to a lot of people. And he'll be remembered in many ways because of that. He touched so many people on both a personal and professional level because of the all-encompassing, time-consuming nature of our business.

Personally, I'll remember him simply as my big brother.

I'll remember him as the guy who was always tousling my hair when I was little. I'll remember him as the young man who came home on leave while in the navy and surprised me by giving me a dollar—which I thought was the neatest thing in the world at the time.

Because there was such a big age separation between us, he remained a big brother figure to me right up to the end of his life. He watched over me in a lot of ways through the years, first as simply a brother and eventually as a colleague in our business operations.

I grew up following his examples in a lot of areas, personally and professionally, and that was always fine with me. The examples he set invariably made a lot of sense in whatever area you were dealing. He had this innate intelligence that always seemed to steer things in the right direction, ultimately.

Basically, he was smart as a whip, and I always felt good about myself when an opinion of mine coincided with what he thought about something. Luckily for me, I got to experience that sort of feeling a lot.

Something that developed over time that I found interesting was that people could often go ask Bill a question, then later on ask me the same question and get basically the same answer. Perhaps that was because of both Mom and Dad hammering the same stuff into us for so many years.... I don't know. But something stuck with us, I think. Bill and I seemed to always have the same approach to a lot of things. That's probably because of how much I learned from him on a day-to-day basis.

We had a really unique, really special relationship. We both had our strengths, but I always considered him a mentor. And I knew he always had my best interests at heart. We complemented each other. I know that he definitely complemented me and kept me going in the right direction when I was growing up.

I think there are a lot people in the world who have inherited something considerable and successful—and then squandered it. I hope that people will remember Bill as someone who didn't do that. He ran in the other direction, becoming totally dedicated to taking what Mom and Dad started and not squandering what he had been given a chance to develop. He kept it going, kept building it, and made it better. That sort of thing doesn't happen a lot.

His dedication had a lot of roots in simplicity, which are well-documented in this book's preceding pages.

He was accessible, coming to work every day, year after year. He was grounded despite his successes. He knew that he put his pants on the same way as everyone else did—he never forgot that.

As you've read elsewhere in these pages, he was impressed by no one—starting with himself. And, in a roundabout way, that is what made Bill France Jr. so extraordinary.

I have been proud to call him my brother for as long as I can remember. There is not a day that goes by when I don't miss his counsel, even if that meant he might be giving me hell about something.

With Bill France Jr., you had what you could call a real straight-shooter.

And almost always, his aim was pretty good.

Chronology

Bill France Jr.—A Life Timeline

- April 4, 1933: William Clifton France is born in Washington, D.C., the son of William H.G. France and Anne Bledsoe France.
- October 1934: The France family arrives in Daytona Beach, Florida, and makes it their home.
- October 24, 1944: Brother, James C. France is born in Daytona Beach, Florida.
- June 7, 1951: Graduates from Seabreeze High School in Daytona Beach, Florida.
- 1951–52: Attends the University of Florida.
- 1953–55: Serves in the United States Navy.
- 1956: Goes to work for his father at Bill France Racing, Inc., the predecessor of International Speedway Corporation.
- 1957: Becomes director of courses for NASCAR.
- September 20, 1957: Weds Betty Jane Zachary of Winston-Salem, North Carolina.
- 1958: Named assistant race director for NASCAR.
- 1959: Named member of the board of directors of the new Daytona International Speedway.
- 1960: Named track superintendent of Daytona International Speedway.
- May 24, 1961: Daughter, Lesa France (Kennedy), is born in Daytona Beach, Florida.
- 1962: Named general manager of Daytona International Speedway.
- August 2, 1962: Son, Brian Zachary France, is born in Daytona Beach, Florida.
- 1963: Named vice president of Daytona International Speedway.

- 1966: Named vice president of NASCAR.
- November 1971: Competes in the Baja 1000 riding a motorcycle, continuing an amateur career as an enduro rider.
- January 10, 1972: Named the second president of NASCAR, replacing his father.
- 1972: Oversees reduction of NASCAR Winston Cup Series schedule to 31 races, all on paved tracks.
- February 1974: Shortens Daytona 500 to 450 miles to show support for fuel crisis.
- 1976: The NASCAR Winston Cup Series takes the lead in worldwide motorsports attendance at 1.4 million spectators.
- February 18, 1979: First live flag-to-flag coverage of the Daytona 500, by CBS Sports.
- 1981: Named chief operating officer of newly formed International Speedway Corporation (ISC).
- 1981: Moves the NASCAR Winston Cup Series Awards Ceremony from Daytona Beach, Florida, to New York City.
- 1982: ISC purchases historic Darlington Raceway in South Carolina.
- 1983: ISC purchases interest in Watkins Glen International road course in upstate New York.
- 1989: For the first time, every event in NASCAR's premier series is televised.
- June 7, 1992: Father, William H.G. (Big Bill) France dies.
- August 6, 1994: The inaugural Brickyard 400 at Indianapolis Motor Speedway is held.
- February 1995: The first event for the NASCAR Craftsman Truck Series is held at Phoenix International Raceway.
- 1995: NASCAR.com is launched through a partnership between NASCAR and ESPN Internet Ventures.
- 1996: International Speedway Corporation becomes 12 percent equity owner of Penske Motorsports, Inc.
- July 5, 1996: DAYTONA USA, "The Ultimate Motorsports Attraction," opens to the public at Daytona International Speedway.
- April 1997: ISC acquires remaining interest in Watkins Glen International.
- July 1997: ISC acquires Phoenix International Raceway.
- 1998: NASCAR celebrates its 50th anniversary and names its 50 Greatest Drivers.

- 1998: ISC named to *Forbes* list of 200 Best Small Companies in America.
- October 1998: Daytona International Speedway holds first NASCAR night race.
- February 1999: Names Mike Helton as NASCAR chief operating officer.
- July 1999: ISC completes merger with Penske Motorsports, Inc., acquiring four tracks—Auto Club Speedway, Michigan International Speedway, North Carolina Speedway, and Nazareth Speedway.
- November 11, 1999: NASCAR signs $2.4 billion television deal with FOX, NBC, and Turner Sports to begin in 2001.
- December 1999: ISC acquires Richmond International Raceway.
- January 2000: R.J. Reynolds announces increase of NASCAR Winston Cup Series point fund from $5 to $10 million, with the champion's share increasing to $3 million.
- November 28, 2000: Names Mike Helton new NASCAR president; becomes chief executive officer and chairman of newly created NASCAR board of directors.
- 2001: Named International Entrepreneur of the Year by the University of Missouri–KC.
- October 2001: ISC acquires remaining 10 percent of Homestead-Miami Speedway.
- January 2003: The $10 million NASCAR Research & Development Center in Concord, North Carolina, is unveiled.
- 2003: Bill France passes the role of ISC CEO to brother, James C. France.
- 2003: Lesa France Kennedy becomes president of ISC.
- June 19, 2003: Announces Sprint Nextel as new sponsor of NASCAR's premier series, ending a 33-year relationship with R.J. Reynolds.
- October 2003: Replaced as NASCAR chairman/CEO by son, Brian Z. France; assumes new role as NASCAR vice-chairman.
- January 2004: NASCAR announces the Chase for the NASCAR Sprint Cup, a championship format dividing the season into a 26-race preseason and a 10-race late-season schedule to determine the season champion.
- May 2004: Inducted into the International Motorsports Hall of Fame in Talladega, Alabama.
- May 2004: ISC acquires Martinsville Speedway, sells North Carolina Speedway.
- June 2004: Inducted into the Motorsports Hall of Fame of America in Novi, Michigan.

- October 2004: Inducted into the Motorcycle Hall of Fame in Pickerington, Ohio.
- December 2005: NASCAR announces $4.5 billion television deal with FOX, ABC, ESPN, TNT, and SPEED to begin in 2007.
- October 2006: Inducted into the Automotive Hall of Fame in Midland, Michigan.
- June 4, 2007: Dies at his home in Daytona Beach, Florida, at the age of 74.

Index